# Wisdom
## — For Days

## BRYAN PHARR

WISDOM – FOR DAYS by Bryan Pharr

Published by IEXIST Publishing

This book or parts thereof may not be reproduced in any form, stored in a retrieval system or transmitted in any form by any means – electronic, mechanical, photocopy, recording or otherwise – without prior written permission of the publisher, except as provided by United States of America copyright law.

Copyright © 2021 by Bryan Pharr
All rights reserved

ISBN 978-0-578-84178-6

Thank you to my mother and wife who inspired at least two of these quotes.

# TO THE READER:

Firstly, thank you so much for purchasing this copy of "Wisdom – For Days". Every piece of wisdom found in this book was either learned through experience or earned through painful experiences. Because of this, I consider all of the information held within these pages as valuable and trustworthy – and so should you.

I encourage you to read at least one key per day until you've finished the entire book. And don't just read it. I also encourage you to take a moment to write out how each quote or wisdom key is speaking to you individually, whether in a separate notebook or directly on these pages. It's yours to decide.

Lastly, I encourage you to share what you're learning and the keys that most speak to you. But because these are original quotes and keys, be sure to give credit where it's due ;)

Enjoy!

# WISDOM
# -
# FOR DAYS

## "

# Fulfillment doesn't come from changing into things you aren't but rather from becoming all that you are.

(For days when you need to be reminded of who you are)

You are a "finished seed". You've been fully God-stocked with everything you need for life and fulfillment since birth…An apple seed will not find fulfillment in attempting to become a pear tree. A dandelion seed cannot find fulfillment in attempting to become a rose bush. In the same way, your fulfillment in life will come from becoming everything you were designed and intended to be. The fruit of fulfillment follows bold alignment with who you are and belief in who you are.

Bryan Pharr

> **Confidence comes in knowing that there's only one person who can play the role you've been given in this life – and that's you. There's no one better for the part.**

(For days when you need to be reminded of just how valuable and unique you are)

You have no competition for who it is you're called to be. Your uniqueness sets you apart from the rest for the specific intention and purpose you were born into this world for. There is no one better to accomplish what it is you were created to fulfill. We are all as unique as the snowflakes that fall to the earth in the winter – all of the same substance, but all shaped differently, predestined to make a never-duplicated impression on the earth.

"

**A fear of what people may think of you will always prevent you from being who you need to be for yourself and for them.**

(For days when you need to be bold)

Not setting out to do things that you know you should do for fear of people's views and opinions changing of you is the quickest way to trap yourself in the misery of stagnation. To not grow, progress or discover and do the things that make you happy is not only a disservice to yourself but also to everyone you are capable of positively affecting in this world. Of course, as with everything else in life, there IS a cost to changing for the better. But a wasted life is much more costly than one that embraces betterment.

**Bryan Pharr**

"

# Don't let anyone get between you and your responsibility to be a gift to the world around you.

(For days when you need to remember why you're here)

It can be easy to get caught up in the hustle and bustle of maintaining our livelihoods while ensuring that the agendas of those we love and are responsible to be fulfilled. These things, not always requiring us to use our gift(s)/talent(s)/passion, will often cause us to forget our duty to use our innate, natural abilities in acts of service for the betterment of humanity. Sometimes while helping everyone else to shine around us, we'll dim, hide or even smother out our own light, neglecting our responsibility to be a light to those around us and ultimately forsake our purpose in being here on earth. Shine.

"

# You can't change what you don't face.

(For days when you need to be brave)

Often, many of the situations we consider to be insurmountable or impossible to change are simply issues we haven't faced and have fearfully projected negative outcomes toward. Even when change is hard, determinedly facing what needs to change in our lives will cause us to realize the immeasurable strength that was latent within us to effectively change and overcome our current, negative circumstances the entire time.

"

# Never put your destiny in the hands of another. Be responsible for your own life.

(For days when your expectation of someone "helping" you has been let down)

No one is responsible for ensuring that your dreams come true but you. You are fully equipped with the ability to see them through to manifestation. The pain of "let-down" in your life could very well be coming from the misconception that someone else is supposed to **GIVE** you what you are intended to **GROW**.

"

# You have everything you need - inside.

(For days when you need to be reminded that you are enough)

Everything you need to flourish in the earth is already in you.

Bryan Pharr

"

# Challenge your convictions…

(For days when you need to get uncomfortable so that you can grow)

…especially those that aren't rooted by knowledge and understanding. It is very possible that you could be missing out on your best life by being directed and controlled by misguiding, hearsay-driven convictions. Be a student. If you don't know why you believe something, learn why. Don't allow your life's potential to be capped by empty, unproductive beliefs that do more to hold you back than empower you.

"

# Your life awaits your decision.

(For days when you need to be reminded of your power to make a choice)

Your ability to make decisions is one of the greatest tools you have in this life. Life doesn't **MAKE** you be great; you choose to be. Life, in the same way, won't **MAKE** you a failure either. You'd have to choose that also. The direction of your life is always set by your decisions and not the other way around. You shouldn't be waiting on life to make you decide because life, is awaiting **YOUR** decision.

Bryan Pharr

"

# You'll win if you don't quit.

(For days when you need to be reminded of the way to win)

Something quite beautiful about this life is that it was designed in a way that we can ALL win. As a matter of fact, you've already won. You aren't being pitted against the rest of all humanity for a limited supply of gain. There is more than enough for the prosperity, peace and happiness of every single person alive. There is truly no competition. The strength or pace of anyone else's life performance has absolutely nothing to do with you winning. This "race" is only one of faith, love and endurance.

# Wisdom – For Days

"

# You'll never fully pursue what you're made for until you learn to hate what you settle for.

(For days when you need to see the purpose of the pain in the places you ought not to remain)

Pain and experience are sometimes the best teachers. They allow you to learn to hate what you settle for so that you can pursue your best and never return.

Bryan Pharr

**"**

# Your crucifixion is just a means to your crown.

(For days when you need to be reminded to take the high road)

It can be emotionally overwhelming and utterly discouraging to have to go through seasons in life of being wrongfully accused and sentenced by those who plot and take joy in your downfall - for seemingly no reason at all. There may not be a more accurate depiction of or metaphor for these moments in time than an unjust murder in the form of crucifixion. If it is you who is facing this character assassination born from jealousy and hate, endure. Take the high road, avoiding any need to get even or to pay back hate for hate, because your crucifixion is just a means to your crown.

"

# The right time to be better is always now.

(For days when you need the courage to change)

As soon as you know better, be better. You may pay a cost for "separating yourself from the pack" by deciding to be different than what those who surround you are used to. But it will never truly serve you or them to stay the same when you could be better.

**Bryan Pharr**

"

# Don't be afraid to learn from people who don't look like you.

(For days when you need to be reminded to be open-minded)

If you qualify the gift by the packaging it comes in, you'll often throw away what's invaluable because of what, to you, looks worthless. Whether across cultural, age, ethnic, sex, social, economic, political or religious lines, it's important to have enough humility to be able to learn from those who you may not naturally expect to have answers you need. This does not mean that you should take in everything everyone says as factual, but rather that you shouldn't limit who you can learn through. Limited sources ultimately result in limited resource.

"

# Show them that you believe in you.

(For days when you need to let go of your need for others' approval)

Don't waste time trying to get others to believe in you. Show them that you believe in you and those who are willing to follow suit will. The reality is that if you need others to believe in you first in order to progress, you may never move forward in the direction you wish to go. Most who come to believe in you will (eventually) only attach themselves to the results of the belief you've had in yourself over a long period of time. They will need proof. You will need to believe in yourself when there is none.

Bryan Pharr

**"**

# Don't let their assessment become your limitation.

(For days when you need to break the chains of what "they" say)

Don't allow people to limit how far you can go concerning what you've been designed to do. If you're willing to put in the work to get there, you can go as far as you want to go.

"

# If they're your friends only when they think you're winning, they aren't true friends.

(For days when you need to reassess your friendships)

Bought friends aren't real friends.

Bryan Pharr

**"**

**If they're your friends only when they feel they're doing better than you, they aren't true friends.**

(For days when you need to reassess your friendships)

Don't mistake "being used" as real friendship.

"

## Longevity in relationship is the proof of genuine investment.

(For days when you need to be reminded not to give up on people)

Never stop genuinely and pure-heartedly (without pretense for self gain) investing in others. Sometimes after being hurt, it's possible to allow distrust to prevent us from investing in those we need to - all the while cutting short what's sometimes meant to be long lasting. Investments don't die.

**Bryan Pharr**

## "

# Self-confidence without self-awareness leads to self-sabotage.

(For days when you need to own up to who you really are)

When you're more concerned about portraying an image to fit in with others rather than being your authentic and best self, you'll always cut yourself short of your destiny. Talking a good game can only get you so far. Eventually others will meet the person behind what's being portrayed by words. Most of us who talk more than we act are actually afraid to act, knowing that we may not be who we portray ourselves to be. Be yourself. Get to know yourself. Grow yourself. Lasting self-confidence can only be based in truth.

"

# Their dream, their job…

(For days when you need to go your own way)

Don't waste time obligating yourself to fulfilling what others wished they had done. After seeing what may be considered as potential, there are some people that may attempt to force their unmet aspirations and dreams on you. Their desire is to reach their goals vicariously through you and as a result, will often suck up any glory for any positive outcomes by crediting themselves for making you who you've become. We all have a responsibility towards our own dreams and potential. Live out yours.

> **Learn to take the fast lane sometimes. Learn from others.**

(For days when you feel lost)

If you aren't making new mistakes, chances are you're making some of the same mistakes those who have gone before you have made. It's ok to look at their successes and mimic their faith, including some of their strategy if it's conducive to your success within your personal journey. It's also ok to look at their failures and learn what not to do and where not to go. It isn't necessary for you to have to learn everything "the hard way" when you can stand on the shoulders and lessons of those who have walked the steps you are about to take. Not all advice is good advice, but there is certainly safety in a multitude of counsel. There are no shortcuts to true success. But you don't have to stay in the lane of the lost.

"

# Plenty chase the spotlight, but it's the heroes who chase the darkness – because they are the light.

(For days when you need to be reminded of how to truly be effective in this life)

It isn't those who run after the spotlight in an attempt to make themselves look big who are the real heroes. It is those who use their light (on the inside) to bring an end to the darkness around them.

Bryan Pharr

"

# What's trending isn't always what's true.

(For days when you need to ground yourself in the truth)

Fine-tune your ears and mind to only receive truth so that you aren't swayed by every story that comes your way. Sooner or later we all have to embrace enough individuality to be responsible for what we personally intake and believe. Just because it's trending, doesn't mean it's always true. Arguing, being divided, and making major mistakes because of hearsay information or trending opinion shouldn't be an option. Don't always take the lazy route. Learn to be in community with others and still cultivate a trust in your own intuition, voice and ability to learn and grow on your own. Have your own mind.

"

# It's never too late to begin again.

(For days when you need to be reminded not to waste the gift that is a new day)

Every sunrise you witness is an indication of a new opportunity and another chance.

Bryan Pharr

**"**

# Your greatest fear is often the single barrier in front of your greatest blessing.

(For days when you need to be reminded to defy your fears)

Get out of your comfort zone.

"

# Your freedom is vital to the fulfillment of your purpose.

(For days when you need to fight for your freedom)

In order to walk in your purpose and see it through, you must be free enough to be yourself.

Bryan Pharr

"

# Your enemies don't have as much power as they think they do.

(For days when you need to take your power back)

Those who believe they can completely control the outcome of your life are only kidding themselves. They only have as much power as you give them.

"

# Don't be afraid to let go of what you thought was true.

(For days when you need to be ok with moving on)

Some of the hardest junctures to navigate on the road to progression and growth are those that require you to accept that some things that you saw as truth thus far weren't true at all. There can be an associated fear with finding out that what you believed (or trusted) about something or someone, whether through ignorance, pride or avoidance, isn't what it seemed or presented itself to be. Out of fear, we often prolong the process of growth and progress by now entering a state of denial concerning what we've just found out to be true. The truth is, finding out that you thought wrong is a part of growth too. And when the truth is revealed, it's often for your protection and always for your direction.

Bryan Pharr

"

# Make sure your fight stays on the outside.

(For days when you need to be sure that you're in the right fight)

When you're living out your life's purpose, you'll have an inward peace but you'll often have to fight elements on the outside of you that seek to stop you or to deter you from that purpose. When you abandon your purpose, falling to the pressures of those outside elements, conforming to a lesser effective person than you were intended to be, your fight becomes with yourself. Either way, you'll always have a fight. But a fight with yourself on the inside is the only one that can destroy your destiny. Be sure YOUR fight stays on the outside. There's strength for that fight. You'll win if you don't let it in.

XXX

"

# Your worth isn't determined by what you can do for others.

(For days when you feel rejected)

Even with the best intentions behind your actions, it can be hard not to associate your worth with how valuable others perceive you. Your worth was and is established by your Creator and is an intrinsic value that was instituted before you ever realized your own existence. Apart from other people, you're worth more than anything in this universe that a human could trade for your time or work. Whether or not someone acknowledges that fact or personally sees you as valuable has no bearing on that actual reality.

Bryan Pharr

"

# Gratefulness is an indicator that you can handle more.

(For days when you feel overwhelmed with work)

Although life at times can present a set of burdensome circumstances that are meant to prove that you have more strength than you initially thought, feeling overly burdened can also be an indicator that you may be playing the wrong position in life. You'll notice that certain positions and responsibilities that some people are grateful for, others perceive as "burdens". This is often a sign that you may not be graced to play that particular part. Life will become burdensome for everyone at certain junctures - it's a part of growth. But the key here is to recognize when the overbearing weight of a certain position or role is meant to push you out and ultimately into alignment with your specific purpose.

"

# Life is found through purpose, not in possessions.

(For days when you need to adjust your priorities)

Riches can't fill the emptiness of the soul that has not found purpose. They can, however, aid the purpose of the one who has found life.

Bryan Pharr

**"**

# The world doesn't know it needs you until you unveil and avail your gift(s).

(For days when you feel ineffective)

Your gift(s) (your true, latent talents/ability) are an answer for someone somewhere. But they may never know it unless you uncover and put them to use.

"

# Your worth isn't determined by your circumstances.

(For days when your momentary circumstances have discouraged you)

When your worth is anchored in the truth of who you really are (i.e. great, powerful, necessary, triumphant, loved, etc.), life's circumstances aren't allowed to alter how you feel about yourself. Contentment can live where worth is constant. It allows you to be authentic and remain consistent right where you are, not having to pretend as if things were different.

Bryan Pharr

"

# Don't waste your experiences. Learn to use them all.

(For days when you need to see the purpose in the burden AND in the blessing)

Don't allow bitterness, hatred and self-pity to be lasting results of bad experiences in life. Forgive. These are often the times that make you the most relatable to others.
Don't allow complacency, pride and greed to creep in from the good that happens in your life. Keep giving. These are often the times when you have the greatest ability to help those around you.

"

# Parenthood isn't about delegation. It's about duplication.

(For days when you need to be reminded of the priority of parenthood)

Cold instruction alone leaves a child with a false image of the parent and starts a lifelong cycle of attempting to be validated, accepted and loved through pleasing the parent – sometimes by any means necessary. It also inhibits growth (or maturity). Parenthood is meant to be a loving transfer of heart through the vehicles of:

- Leadership - being an example
- Exposure - showing the real you &
- Vulnerability - putting your heart on the line

Bryan Pharr

**"**

# Life will meet the need you create.

(For days when you need to step into the unknown)

Faith is about creating a need and, while working, joyfully expecting life to meet it. If you would dare step out, you'll find that life has already made provision to hold you up.

"

**Immediate sacrifice leads to long-term satisfaction, but immediate satisfaction leads to long-term sacrifice.**

(For days when you need to really take advantage of your now)

We often suffer long-term for the sacrifices we won't make today. Learn to embrace discipline, endurance, personal responsibility, humility, unconditional love and other "sacrificial" qualities early so that the sacrifice of your today can produce the satisfaction of your tomorrow.

Bryan Pharr

"

# You're a solution to the problem that bothers you the most.

(For days when you need help locating your purpose)

You can often discover purpose through the problem(s) that, sometimes, only you see. It's the situations that bother us, pull on our heartstrings and call us to action that can lead us to our purpose.

"

# You're meant to overcome what's overcoming you.

(For days when you need to find the strength to fight)

Many times we're asking to be relieved of what we're meant to overcome. Some battles come into your life to prove to you that the grace and strength to win was within you even before you entered the fight.

# "

# It's not what you learn. It's what you know.

(For days when you need help locating your gift)

One of the foundational indications of whether a skill you have is your God-given gift or not is that it will always be a talent you didn't have to learn to do. The knowledge of how it operates will be tied to it. You'll simply understand it without the help of any outside voice. This doesn't mean that it doesn't need to be developed or worked in order to see your potential emerge. It also doesn't mean that learning won't enhance your gift. But there is a difference between developing what's already there and trying to grow something that hasn't been planted.

"

# Spirituality isn't the opposite of productivity.

(For days when you feel pressured by or guilty because of the religious order)

You don't have to spend all day in trance-like meditation in order to be considered spiritual. When viewed and received properly, healthy spirituality should actually enhance and multiply your productivity.

Bryan Pharr

"

# Own your purpose.

(For days when you need to fully take responsibility for why it is that you're here)

No one can own it for you and no amount of external validation of it will bring long-term satisfaction. It feels great if others see potential in you and/or believe in you, which isn't always the case. But until you believe in your purpose and live it out, you won't experience the freedom and fulfillment that accompanies it.

"

# Expect good things.

(For days when you need to rid yourself of negative expectations)

Make a decision to only expect good things to happen in your life. Even when bad things happen – and they will – expect good to come out of them. Do this, not because you're so perfect, but because you're worth it.

Bryan Pharr

"

# Contentment makes way for what you need.

(For days when you need to cut the distractions that are preventing you from getting what you need)

The anxiety associated with trying to attain what you think you want often blocks you from being able to see what you actually need. Contentment or peace with who you are, where you are and what you currently have makes way for what you would've wanted had you known you needed it in the first place.

# Don't trade your light for the spotlight.

(For days when you need to remember just how valuable "the real you" is)

Trading your authenticity, uniqueness, purpose and effectiveness for any amount of shallow fame or popularity is always a bad deal.

Bryan Pharr

**"**

# Stop trying to make sense and make a move.

(For days when you need to take a leap of faith)

Faith has always involved risk. It's believing even when you can't physically see "it". It's knowing something is on the other side of your situation even though you haven't been there yet. It's walking when you don't quite know how to get where you're going but are assured of your destination. You may not ever be able to make taking a leap of faith make sense, especially to others. Do it anyway.

"

## Investing in others begins with investing in you.

(For days when you need to take care of yourself first)


Your capacity to invest in others will be limited to the investment and love you have received or given yourself both inwardly and outwardly.

Bryan Pharr

**"**

# Choosing life is a full-time job. I don't have time for part-time negativity.

(For days when you need to cut the negativity out of your life)

When choosing to really live, you don't have time to be negative.

"

**Faith will never have you to embark on a journey that Grace hasn't already seen you through.**

(For days when you're unsure of whether you have enough to make it through)

Your faith will never lead you down a path that you have not already been empowered and equipped to walk. When the way gets rough, tests you at every turn and you become uncertain of whether you have what it takes; just remember that you were pre-stocked with everything you could need to see your journey through.

Bryan Pharr

"

# Don't let the pain keep you from the promise.

(For days when you need to hold on)

Endure.

"

# Pressure corrects posture.

(For days when you need to see the point of the pressure)

Life's pressures have a way of correcting our posture. They reveal a posture of strength in the weak and produce one of humility in the overly proud.

Bryan Pharr

"

# You're worthy of the life that was intended for you.

(For days when you need to realize that you're worthy)

When we settle for less than the life that was meant for us – one that is full of fulfillment – it is often an indication of our perceived self-worth. You're worthy of a life that exceeds your "wildest" dreams.

"

# You can if you will.

(For days when you need to give in to your dream)

You've already been given the capacity and the capability to fulfill your dream. All your dream needs now is your compliance.

Bryan Pharr

"

# Assumptions cloud judgment.

(For days when you need to make a decision)

Get clarity before you act or make that decision. Any blind spot that is left to your imagination to fill in missing information becomes grounds for you to assume the wrong thing – which often leads to major mistakes being made. Don't assume. Assess.

"

## Create your own space.

(For days when you need to break the mold)

You aren't obligated to do what's been done. Don't kill the dream just because it hasn't been done before.

Bryan Pharr

**"**

# Don't trade your blessing for their burden.

(For days when you need to rid yourself of the manipulator)

How often do we forsake our own calling in exchange for someone else's agenda for our lives? Don't trade the blessing of walking in your purpose for distractions disguised as opportunities or needs of you from others that come to derail you from your calling and destiny.

"

## Life is less about ascension and more about relation.

(For days when you need to remember that you didn't get here alone)

It gets hard to set ourselves apart as "higher than others" when we realize that, no matter how hard we've worked, we didn't get where we are without someone looking out for us, giving us a chance, sharing insight, knowledge, or wisdom with us, sacrificing for us or lending us a hand.

Bryan Pharr

"

# Don't give room to yesterday's mistakes in today's miracles.

(For days when you need to let the past go)

Forgiving yourself includes realizing that yesterday's mishaps are the building blocks for today's miracles. You can drop the guilt in knowing that you wouldn't have had "this" miracle without that "mess".

"

# Speak well until it gets well.

(For days when you need to change what you're saying)

Your words have transformative power over you. You have transformative power over your situation.

Bryan Pharr

"

# Celebrate the people who go before you.

(For days when you need to be grateful that you have an example)

Celebrate the people who walk in your line of purpose that went before you. Don't hate on the people who are doing what you aspire to do. You attract what you respect.

"

# The ones who oppose your promotion are often the ones who didn't witness your process.

(For days when you have to face the fact that not everyone likes it when you win)

Don't worry about the ones who don't believe you should be where you are. Stand tall knowing that true promotion is developed from within and that it didn't come without the proper process.

Bryan Pharr

"

# Don't underestimate your ability to positively affect the world around you.

(For days when you need to stop doubting yourself)

Your part to play is bigger than you think.

Wisdom – For Days

"

# Pride causes you to compete with what/who you were meant to support.

(For days when you need to trade competition for collaboration)

You're better together.

**Bryan Pharr**

**"**

# Do it for your own applause.

(For days when you feel you aren't getting the support you need)

At first, you may not be applauded for chasing your dreams.
Do it for your own applause.

"

# You cannot become your best self apart from love.

(For days when you need to be reminded that love is the way)

Love is the glue and foundation that ties us to true success. When your actions proceed out of love for self and those around you, you ignite the potential to do more than you ever could have done working from a place of hatred, pride or obligation.
"The lovers will always outwork the workers." – John Crowder

Bryan Pharr

"

## Just enough is never enough.

(For days when you need to be reminded to give it all you've got)

You get out of it what you put into it.

"

# Even with nothing, you're more than enough.

(For days when you need to be reminded of where the value really is)

Your success has never been predicated upon outside resources. When you learn to see the intrinsic value and worth you have as a human, you'll realize that even with nothing, you have more than enough to see every dream you have come to fruition.

Bryan Pharr

"

**Authenticity is not an excuse for stagnancy. Don't let your best you fall victim to a lesser you.**

(For days when you need to cut ties with who you used to be)

Don't let where you're from and where you started be the final say concerning where you can go. Authenticity is the basis for true development, not an excuse to "be real" and stay where you are. The best you IS the real you.

"

# Don't just use your imagination to escape your reality. Use it to change your reality.

(For days when you need to do something about the dream)

Most spend their days using their imagination to dream about "what would happen or what could happen if"…instead of using it to decide what will happen. Work the dream. Make it live.

Bryan Pharr

"

**A mind to be king may make you a slave. A mind to be a servant will make you a king.**

(For days when you need to be reminded of what a real queen's/king's heart looks like)

A heart to serve is a King's/Queen's heart.

"

# On the way to where you're going, take time to remember how far you've come.

(For days when you need a reason to be thankful)

You don't have to wait until your next completed step to be grateful. Be thankful for the last.

Bryan Pharr

"

# You're best day is never behind you.

(For days when you need to value your "now")

When you learn to value and use all of the wisdom, knowledge and growth you have or can gain through all of your past experiences, you'll begin to realize that yesterday does not have to be your best day. You have all of the tools to continually make "now" the best time of your life.

"

# You can't be confused about the calling you were willing to chase.

(For days when you just need to make a move)

The longer you wait to go after that dream or calling, the more "confusion" will start to set in. You'll begin to excuse yourself for procrastinating and for being unwilling to pursue your purpose. Taking steps toward your calling is what irons out the details that you would love to know before you begin to walk it out. But chasing requires faith. Learning by failing and taking risks is a part of the process. The quicker you comply with the calling, the faster the confusion will begin to dissipate. It can't live where faith has caused you to take action.

Bryan Pharr

"

# Believe, even if you're counted out.

(For days when you need to hold on a little longer and not compromise)

It may sound simple, but I believe it would stop so many of us from making bad choices in times of desperation. No matter how bad it's gotten, if you're down to your last, or backed into a corner, there's nothing that can be done to you that compares to what faith can do for you.

# You become what you behold.

(For days when you need to get out and go see something different)

Exposure is one of the greatest assets to identity. We learn from and become what we consistently see. Sometimes making a change in our lives is as simple as changing what we are constantly exposing ourselves to.

Bryan Pharr

**"**

# You're strong enough for the fight you're in.

(For days when you need encouragement in the fight)

You aren't facing anything you weren't built for.
You aren't facing anything you can't overcome.

"

# Are you willing to pay for what you've prayed for?

(For days when you need to confront your comfort in order to grow)

Not too many of us typically have a problem with "greater" or "better". Receiving what we pray for alone isn't necessarily what costs us. The cost is associated with what we have to let go of. Being unwilling to let go of the habits, hurts, fears, comfortability, assurance, people, attitudes, ideas or perceptions that hinder true reception is often the blockade to our blessing.

Bryan Pharr

"

**Hope is the invisible light that gives faith permission to set our feet in motion, even in the darkest night.**

(For days when you need to keep hope alive)

Hope isn't a delusion that keeps us still. It's the type of expectation that fuels our movement.

# Faith jumps first.

(For days when you need to take a healthy risk)

You don't have time to figure it all out. Prepare as best as you can and take the leap. Faith takes the leap and trusts that you'll figure it out along the way.

Bryan Pharr

**"**

# You haven't lived until you've lived for another.

(For days when you need to step out of selfishness into selflessness)

If you want to live fulfilled, you'll need to understand its giving and reciprocal nature. Until you have come to the place that you can willingly live to serve others through your gifts or aptitudes, you cannot know the sweet fruit of living fulfilled.

Wisdom – For Days

"

# If you can see the purpose you can endure the pain.

(For days when you need to find or remember your reason to fight on)

It can be plenty difficult to last through seasons of tumultuous circumstances in your life – especially when it seems everything you're going through is happening for no reason at all. But if you can see the purpose in what you're fighting through or see your victorious end before it comes to be, you'll find that lasting through the trial will be multiplied times easier than it would be if you had no reason to. Endure.

Bryan Pharr

**"**

# Being your best means fighting the pressure to be like the rest.

(For days when you need to resist the urge to compromise who you are)

Dimming your own light for anyone else's comfort will lead you into a life of discomfort and leave your destiny abandoned.

"

# Love as if you won't have an opportunity to tomorrow.

(For days when you need to love harder)

Take the risk. Put your heart on the line. Don't take for granted what could only last for a limited amount of time.

Bryan Pharr

**"**

# Don't expect people to see in you what they can't see in themselves.

(For days when you're short on encouragement from others)

Stop seeking encouragement of the greatness in you from those who can't see greatness in themselves. How can someone identify what they don't yet recognize? Learn to encourage yourself.

"

# At some point, you're going to have to decide whether you're hated or loved.

(For days when you need to leave the land of limbo)

The truth is, you're loved. But I believe most of us constantly switch between the two. When something great happens, we believe we're loved and life is for us. When something bad happens, we believe we're hated and that the entire universe is against us. There are a few of us though, who realize that life is for us and are able to see good coming, even through the toughest situations. They know they are loved and that life is happening for them, not to them, no matter the circumstance. My advice to you is to take the side of the few.

Bryan Pharr

**"**

# Your outlook determines your output.

(For days when you need to change the way you see it)

Not only is your interaction with the world around you tied to how you view yourself, it is also affected by how you were taught and have learned to view the world. Want a more positive and healthy interaction? Receive hope.

"

# There is no security in who you pretend to be.

(For days when you need to start moving from insecure to secure)

You were not designed to feel secure while living a lie. Who you really are is enough.

Bryan Pharr

**"**

# If your word matters to you that much, keep the promise you made to yourself.

(For days when you need to finally do what you promised you'd do)

Sometimes significant change doesn't happen in our lives because we're the last person we listen to. Did you promise yourself that you'd make a necessary change? Keep your word – not just for you, but also for everyone tied to you.

"

# The real you will always shine through.

(For days when you need to deal with the root of the issue)

Beautiful things may compliment a beautiful soul, but a bad spirit corrupts beautiful things. No amount of convincing or exterior alteration can mask what's wrong on the inside. "It's the soul that needs the surgery." – Beyoncé

Bryan Pharr

"

**True influence isn't established by building yourself a throne. It is the result of building an altar to sacrifice yourself on for others.**

(For days when you need to be reminded of how to make a true impact)

Thrones decay, but sacrifices will last. What avenue and way have you found or created to help others through? What will they say you built? Find a way to add to people's lives with what you have.

"

**Vulnerability unveils the material with which we either form a bond or we mold bullets to assassinate one another with.**

(For days when you need to be reminded of what it means to be trustworthy)

The gardens of our relationships turn into battlefields when we use the gift of someone's vulnerability as an opportunity to increase our weaponry arsenal and later launch an assault with what they were willing to uncover. Love doesn't do this. Be able to be trusted before asking for someone's trust. Love covers.

Bryan Pharr

"

# The worst excuse to have is the one that says you have it the worst.

(For days when you need to cut the excuses)

There is a real danger in filling in the portions of people's stories we don't know with assumptions – especially those you deem to be successful. Comparing what you assume it took for someone to be where they are to your current situation is often the breeding ground for the excuses we make to stop ourselves from even trying to pursue our purpose. Someone did more with less and went farther with more adversity.

"

# You'll stop selling yourself short for men when you realize that it's God who does the blessing.

(For days when you need to cut the compromise)

Never compromise who you are in order to gain the "blessing" of mankind. You're already blessed. And it's not anyone's fault around you.

Bryan Pharr

**"**

# The truth doesn't need defending. It'll be standing strong long after all the lies have dissipated.

(For days when you need to trust the process)

Don't overly concern yourself with every false accusation against you, even if you've suffered loss because of them. This type of "loss" is normally gain in disguise. Lies are like smoke at best – temporal and fading, attempting only to cover up the truth. It will only expose the accuser in the end.

"

# Sometimes it's your enemy that opens your eyes to your identity.

(For days when you need to appreciate the occasional enemy)

Pay close attention to the people who you may believe are jealous of you "for no reason at all" – especially those who seem threatened by you or who see you as competition. Sometimes it's those that view you as an enemy that saw something in you before a friend or even you could see it in yourself. It's not only those who are for you that can help you identify purpose; it's also those who are against you.

Bryan Pharr

**"**

# Some people say, "I love you", because they actually do.

(For days when you need to let love in)

Don't let manipulators, heartbreakers and the like ruin your ability to recognize and receive from people who genuinely love you unconditionally and without pretense. They do exist. Let love in.

"

**I was lazy concerning my own dreams until I stopped waiting on someone else to help me build them.**

(For days when you need to cut the middleman)

Your dream – your responsibility.

Bryan Pharr

"

# Be more accepting of you.

(For days when you need to appreciate who it is that you are)

You don't need to be anyone else to be significant. Your purpose or role to play in life was already special, unique and significant when it was given to you – but you have to believe that.

"

**Some of you'd be a lot happier if you would learn not to take yourself so seriously.**

(For days when you need to lighten up)


Don't confuse having purpose with having the responsibility to "save the world" – even if you do someday. The truth is that you can't force people to change for the better. But you can always love and try to help them with what helped you, if they allow you to. Lead by example. Don't allow anyone to push you into the type of self-importance that forces you to try to uphold some non-existent standard of perfection – or that causes you to become untouchable and that doesn't allow you to laugh at yourself, have fun or to be human. Enjoy life and solve the problems you were meant to. Purpose is a gift, not a prison.

Bryan Pharr

**"**

# There's more worth in what's in you than in what is on you.

(For days when you need to prioritize you)

Invest more into what's worth more.

"

# Don't overcomplicate the answer you already have.

(For days when you need to drop the excuses)


Sometimes, out of an avoidance or fear of change, we overcomplicate simple answers and solutions we have to present problems in our lives. What overcomplicating simple answers does is make it easier to formulate excuses that "make sense" of why we haven't done what we need to do. What prolonging our process to change with these avoidance techniques does is cause us to suffer longer that we should. Be someone who doesn't have to continually be beat down with "the same old…" before he or she embraces change.

Bryan Pharr

"

**Step so far into the new that it's the old that becomes unfamiliar.**

(For days when going back is an option)

Keep going. Don't look back.

"

# Most of the people you're upset with for not helping you couldn't help you anyway.

(For days when you're frustrated about not having the support you need)

Help yourself. And when real help comes, it'll find you.

"

# You don't always get where you give but you always get what you give.

(For days when you need to unblock your blessings)

Don't allow people who don't reciprocate loving actions or show appreciation for gifts allow you to stop giving. I'm not encouraging you to continue to tie yourself to people who abuse your love or who tolerate you rather than appreciate you. But don't withhold loving actions and generosity from others due to allowing bitterness to set in because of a few people who have mismanaged or taken your gifts for granted. Even when you give without direct reciprocation, what you give will find it's way back to you somehow – whether through personal growth in the form of lessons or through new opportunities, etc., it'll find it's way back.

"

# Taking responsibility for your own life means driving in a world where most only allow themselves to be driven.

(For days when you need to finally take the wheel)

If you're one who keeps wondering why you continually end up in places that you did not want to go in life, the better question to ask may be, "Who's steering (controlling the direction of) my life in the first place?"

Bryan Pharr

**"**

# You're passion is what you're willing to go broke for.

(For days when you need to connect with what really makes you come to life)

If you aren't willing to die for it, you aren't "worthy" to live for it. If you don't love it more than you love money, you probably shouldn't do it.

"

# Let understanding be the reason you listen.

(For days when you need to get along with others around you better)

If you can only hear out who and what you agree with, you're missing out on the greater blessing that comes from listening for understanding. While only listening to see if you agree with what's being said can lead to contention and division, growth and reconciliation can happen if would dare to listen with an intent to understand, whether you agree or not.

Bryan Pharr

"

## Invest – in yourself.

(For days when you need to concern yourself with your own growth)

Nothing grows without care and investment – even you. Could it be that you aren't where you want to be because you're the last person you invest in?

"

## Self-love is not selfish.

(For days when you need to embrace you)

You'll find that the more you're truly
able to love yourself – which is the act of
receiving love – the more capable you
are of truly loving others.

Bryan Pharr

**"**

**Don't waste too much time attempting to tear down negativity. Be the positivity the world needs until what's negative is overturned.**

(For days when you need to focus on being a light)

.

"

# It's not what happens to you but what you identify with that will define you.

(For days when you need to change what you answer to)

No matter the circumstance you may have fallen victim to, you'll be what you identify with. You don't have to be identified as "victim". Be a victor.

Bryan Pharr

**"**

# Don't ask how to win.
# Ask how to lose.

(For days when you need to try it again)

Many of us that don't win, can't win, because we haven't figured out how to lose. If you can't endure the losses, you'll never see the wins. Most losses are only lessons. If you don't learn to see them this way, you'll only count them as failures and reasons to quit. Learn how to lose and you won't ever have to truly lose.

"

**If you have to compromise your character to get it, you'll have to compromise your character to keep it.**

(For days when you need to make the right choice)


Unless you're willing to start all over the right way, how you start is how you'll have to finish. This is #TheProblemWithCompromise.

Bryan Pharr

"

# It's your belief that shapes your behavior.

(For days when you need to get to the root of the issue)

It's not what you say that reveals what you believe. It's how you live. So don't think that you can hide behind empty words intended to help you fit in for long. If you want to really change your reality, you'll have to change at the level of your belief.

"

# Don't get in where you fit in. Get in where you're going.

(For days when you need to get uncomfortable)

If you want better, surround yourself with better. When you allow those who have truly received better for their own lives to inspire you rather than intimidate you, you open the door of possibility to have the same outcome in your own life.

Bryan Pharr

"

**Stop waiting for someone to make you what you won't allow yourself to be.**

(For days when you need to release yourself from the chains of your self-imposed limits)

You don't need permission or to be pushed. You need to be willing.

"

# Feed your dreams and starve your fears.

(For days when you need to change your strategy)

Whatever you don't feed dies.

Bryan Pharr

**"**

# You have an opportunity to live your best life at every waking moment.

(For days when you need to be aware of the mercy within a new day)

Don't take this moment for granted. Every breath is a new chance.

"

## Be sure you aren't chasing your idea of someone else's success.

(For days when you need to be sure that the dream you are chasing is actually yours)

If you spend your life chasing what you're just impressed by and not what you yourself are called to, you run the risk of building or accepting a life you despise. There is no fulfillment in living a life you weren't meant for. Who you are is good enough.

Bryan Pharr

"

# Your self-worth is realized, not attained.

(For days when you need to see your own worth)

It's received not achieved. You're worth more than everything you're trying to attain in order to increase your worth.

"

**Your capacity isn't measured by how much you can hold but rather by how much you can give.**

(For days when you need to be real about the effort you've been putting forth)

What you can have will always be determined by what you can give. What you put into it will determine what you get out of it.

**Bryan Pharr**

"

# Know what you want.

(For days when you need to make a decision)

It's the only way to live intentionally. And living intentionally or on purpose is the only way to live.

"

# I've changed.

(For days when you need to confront those who want you to remain the same)

…Two words you need to be comfortable with if you want to grow. If you don't change, you don't grow. Don't allow anyone to make you feel as if "I've changed" is a derogatory statement. Be the first to admit it.

Bryan Pharr

**"**

# Only today's seed can produce tomorrow's harvest.

(For days when you need to stop wasting time)

The longer you wait, the longer it'll take. A harvest isn't a gift. It's life's response to a seed being sown. Start today.

"

# Stop trying to impress the help.

(For days when you need to accept the help you've been sent)

You'll continue to struggle with those "secret" problems as long as you are too busy trying to conceal them and impress the people who were sent to help you.

Bryan Pharr

"

# If you don't, then who will?

(For days when you need to accept your calling)

Your purpose and call is unique to you and cannot be carried out in the same way by anyone else. Don't allow your purpose to die because of an unwillingness to pursue or fulfill it.

"

**Make certain that the situations that you consider yourself to "have hope in" aren't just situations that you're being stubborn about.**

(For days when you need to be real with yourself)

If everything in and around you is screaming that you need change, don't say to yourself, "I'm staying or standing here in hopes that things will change" (as if by magic). Those things are often signs that we need to change. We change, then our situations change.

Bryan Pharr

"

# Self-discipline isn't just the ability to eliminate the bad. It's also the ability to manage the good.

(For days when you need to gain control over the good that could be killing you)

At certain times in your life, it will be necessary to rid yourself of some things that you've found to only have a negative effect on you – whether food, habits, people, places, etc. But at <u>all</u> times it will be necessary to properly manage the good that remains. If you aren't conscious, even what is good will become bad for you if not given the benefits of self-discipline. Even water, though vital to the health and operation of your body, when drank excessively, can literally become fatal.

"

**Your destiny is dependent upon your change. But you can count on life to sustain you until your change has come.**

(For days when you need to trust that you're taken care of)

Be patient with yourself. Change can be a process. But the process has been provided for.

Bryan Pharr

**"**

**Don't be upset with people who attempt to stop you from being what they won't allow themselves to be. Be free.**

(For days when you need to show empathy and stand your ground)

Misery loves company and bound people bind people. Don't be upset with people who attempt to pull you into their world. Be empathetic and continue to be free.

"

# You are exactly what you've been waiting to see in this world.

(For days when you need to realize you're the answer)

Don't waste another moment saying, "Somebody should…" and waiting on someone else to do it. Go be it!

Bryan Pharr

"

# The problem with trying to prove your worth to everyone is that not everyone deserves your attempt.

(For days when you need to save your energy for the places that matter most)

Don't invite abuse by trying to be something for everyone. "Reserve your worth for those that deserve your worth." Learn early the difference between those who appreciate you and those who only tolerate you.

"

# Don't allow your dreams to die at the hand of a circumstance you have the power to overcome.

(For days when you need to expect more of yourself)

Wouldn't it be something to find out while looking back over a long life of regret that you consistently gave your dreams over to circumstances that you've had the ability to overcome the entire time? Regret isn't the result of climbing a mountain you should have circled. It's the result of circling a mountain you should and could have climbed – it's giving in to what was easy when you had the power to do and accomplish what was hard.

Bryan Pharr

"

**Having faith isn't a substitute for doing the work. It's having enough confidence and assurance in your dreams and visions to work them out.**

(For days when you need to turn fake faith into fruitful faith)

Faith that doesn't work isn't faith at all.

"

# Getting it done isn't nearly as important or rewarding as getting it done the right way.

(For days when you need to do it right the first time)

It's not just what you do but how you do it that will determine the difference between no success, a short-lived success and an "everlasting" one.

Bryan Pharr

**"**

# Some of you aren't winning because you aren't willing to be anyone's enemy.

(For days when you need to be on your own side)

Trying to please everyone or be on everyone's side in order to get ahead will consistently keep you in a cycle of inauthenticity, prevent you from being able to present truth to others and ultimately make failure imminent.

"

# Life will knock the wind out of you. But don't let it beat the belief out of you.

(For days when you need to bounce back)

Keep believing.

Bryan Pharr

"

# There's a difference between being needed and being used.

(For days when you need to be real about your relationships)

So many of us settle for relationships or situations that are sustained by fake, forced, practiced interactions laced with abuse in order to feel as if we're needed, useful, or serving a purpose in life – all while never actually feeling fulfilled or stepping into true purpose. We then often become comfortable with giving off an appearance of fulfillment for our pride's sake rather than taking a loss and actually pushing towards the fulfillment we deserve. This comfort then turns into the type of coping delusion that accepts the abuse of being used as "normal". You're worth more. You deserve the happiness and fulfillment you were made for. But you won't get there faking or settling for anything less.

"

**You've been sold on, fixated on and held back by what's "wrong" with you your entire life. It's time for you to believe in what's "right" with you.**

(For days when you need to change your focus)

No more comparing yourself to others, fixating on what you don't have, believing that those deficiencies are what's "wrong" with you and why you can't live fulfilled. Your specific, unique destiny isn't tied to whatever qualities you see in others that you don't posses. Embrace and love the strengths and qualities you have and you'll find that they're enough for the fulfillment and happiness you sought the entire time.

Bryan Pharr

"

# All of the external motivation and affirmation in the world will mean nothing if you don't believe it.

(For days when you need to believe)

It's your belief that shapes your behavior. It isn't what you or anyone else says that reveals what you believe. It's how you act – intentions included. Those actions determine the trajectory of your life. It won't ever be profitable to surround yourself with positive people, affirmations, and etc. if, in the end, that positivity does not penetrate your belief. Let what is good for you permeate your thoughts until your belief is in line with the positive that's being said.

"

# Change requires change.

(For days that require change of you)

Different actions equal different outcomes.

Bryan Pharr

**"**

# Some of you want friends more than you want freedom.

(For days when you need to choose life over likes)

There's absolutely nothing wrong with having friends. But it's better to have fulfillment with a few than to have misery with many.

"

# Leaders who aren't intent on making you an owner are probably content with owning you.

(For days when you need to give up false hope)

The truth is that there are plenty of task drivers but very few "fathers". The art of fatherhood is duplication – meaning that, for instance, a leader who is a "father" makes other leaders of the people connected to him or her. Most people will never want you to be "as good as them" or better because they do not posses the heart for it. Realistically, you'll always want to carry the weight of your dream on your own shoulders. But ultimately know that if you were to ever come across someone who's heart and intent is to duplicate the good of themself into you, you've found a rare gem.

Bryan Pharr

**"**

# Let yourself live.

(For days when you need to unchain yourself from what you did)

There's no imprisonment like self-imprisonment.

"

# Failure is imminent until it's no longer an option.

(For days when you need to realize your choice in the matter)

You get to choose.

Bryan Pharr

"

**Some of you make your home among the crowds because you can't stand the idea of living with yourself.**

(For days when you need to face yourself)

You'll hide from yourself so that you don't have to be accountable to who you are. You'd rather allow the crowds to define you than to really see who you could be. You're aborting your mission – running from destiny.
Stop running. There's more beauty in you than you could ever imagine.

# If it doesn't manifest, it doesn't matter.

(For days when you need to live the dream)

Stop taking pride in "having a dream". You won't be the first nor the last to say that they have one. What matters most is that you put legs, feet, arms and hands to that dream and actually live it out through your actions. Don't waste anyone else's time talking to them about a dream that you aren't willing to manifest.

Bryan Pharr

"

# Give in to your greatness.

(For days when you need to receive how great you already are)


You don't need to fix yourself.
You need to be yourself.

"

# Emotions are symptoms to manage, not signs to follow.

(For days when you need to take control)

Our emotions are a direct indication of how we are internally processing outside stimuli in the form of experiences. This ultimately means that how we feel is not out of our control. When we change or control our thoughts, adjust our perspective and reason with ourselves so that we can respond instead of react, we in turn grant ourselves the power to shift our emotions. Taking back your power in the area of your emotions begins with realizing that you should be leading your emotions. They shouldn't be leading you.

Bryan Pharr

"

# More important than, "How much can you give?" is life's continual question, "How much will you receive?"

(For days when you need to receive better)

Life is a gift. Will you receive it? Your best gifts will be given reciprocally and out of the gratitude that is formulated when you receive the grace and gifts that are already extended to you daily. Your level of true giving will directly correspond with how much you are willing to receive.

"

# When you compromise for other people's comfort, you keep the world from the best version of you.

(For days when you need to be ok with certain people not liking you)

You aren't doing anyone a favor except those who'd rather see you miserable than at peace or happy when you compromise who you are in order to prevent them from being offended by your greatness.

Bryan Pharr

"

# Your life isn't just about you.

(For days when you need to keep your eyes on the big picture)

Someone needs to see you win.
Someone needs to see you triumph.
Someone needs to see you prosper.
Someone needs to see you overcome.
The quicker you can realize this, the quicker you can begin to recognize that the trials and hardship you're facing aren't all about you either. Don't ever selfishly think that it won't matter if you don't keep going, rise above your current circumstances and live your dreams. Someone is waiting on permission to "be all that they are" and they'll get it when you become.

"

**The journey of success is less about "the destination" and more about who you are when you get there.**

(For days when you need to keep your priorities straight)

You don't get to take anything with you if you decide to leave this life. So your journey better be about more than just accumulating a bunch of things that won't mean anything to you in the end. Those "things" won't save you. You should be focused on who you're becoming, not what you have. What you have will be a byproduct of who you are over time.

Bryan Pharr

**"**

**You're worth too much to put a price on but are too valuable to be wasted.**

(For days when you need to see your worth)

What are you? …

You're a gift.

"

**Even success wouldn't be worth winning if it could not be won authentically.**

(For days when it's just best to do you)

Do yourself a favor:

Be you.
Do you.
Win as you.

Bryan Pharr

"

# Success isn't in knowing someone else. It's in knowing you.

(For days when you need to bet on you)

"They" say, "It's not about what you know, it's about who you know". But too many of us are spending all of our time trying to be "put on" – most ending up being put in prisons made up of other's opinions and designs of what they believe we should be in order to be successful. You end up locked into a character created by those you attempt to be "put on" by, only to eventually realize their disregard for who you are. You'll trade who you are for a fake, lesser version that was truly only intended to bring more "success" to the person or people you've allowed yourself to be controlled by. And even the most well intended opinions are sometimes mere attempts to get you to be what they wish they'd be. I say, "You need to know you", so that you can align yourself with those who can enhance your success rather than dictate it.

"

# I do not define humility as people thinking less of themselves or as thinking of themselves less. Humility is simply one's ability to receive.

(For days when you need to mature)

Humility is not low self-esteem. Humility does not result in a lack of self-awareness. Whether love, correction, praise or instruction, humility is one's ability or willingness to receive it all, no matter the source. This does not mean to receive everything from everybody willingly. What I am emphasizing is that many of you will pridefully reject a gift because of a prejudice or preference that hinders you from getting what you need. The more you can look past the giver or wrapping and receive the gift, the more humility has been worked into your heart.

Bryan Pharr

"

# Life opens up in the direction of your decisions.

(For days when you need to choose better)

Decisions lay the foundation for investment and opportunity. Many of us go through life chasing investments and opportunities, which results in either an unsettled life – jumping from career to career – or either an unhappy life where we'll settle for an unfulfilling career. Decide who it is that you are and what you want first and watch life bring opportunities and investment to you as you pursue purpose.

"

# You rob the world of your greatness when you have a heart to be outstanding but lack a willingness to stand out.

(For days when you need to be brave)

Because of the cost of greatness, many of us avoid its light. But you only rob both the world and yourself when you withhold the very thing that is meant to make you an answer to the needs present in your life – your purpose. You cannot truly be great in private or in silence. Stand out.

Bryan Pharr

**"**

**If you only knew what was ahead of you, you wouldn't be so concerned with what's behind you.**

(For days when you need to let go of the past)

Eyes forward. Your best days are in front of you.

"

# No more playing yourself small. No more selling yourself short. You call that humility. I call it enmity against your own soul.

(For days when you need to step your game up)

The worst enemy you can have is you. Don't allow anyone to talk you into aborting your destiny by turning you against yourself under the guise of "teaching you humility". A lack of confidence and low self-esteem are not traits of humility. Hanging on to those beliefs, no matter where they came from, will cause you to prevent your own success from entering into your life. Be free.

Bryan Pharr

"

**When your progress is no longer predicated upon someone else's approval, you will unchain your life's outcomes from the limits of their desires and expectations.**

(For days when you need to give yourself permission to grow)

Not everyone is going to enjoy seeing you progress in life. If you decide not to move forward until everyone approves of you doing so, you'll often chain yourself to seasons and situations that you've outgrown. This will eventually only prove to make your life and theirs miserable. You don't need their permission to grow. You only need to allow yourself the room.

"

# What you expect affects what you accept.

(For days when you need to up your expectations)

You may believe that low expectations only limit the amount of disappointments you experience, when in reality, you're lowering your standards concerning what you allow into your life. Be careful that you don't allow low expectations to produce a low-level life.

Bryan Pharr

"

**Coming into who you are isn't just an exit from the pain and mediocrity of an inauthentic and suppressed life. It's an entry into the full-blown, fulfilled life that was always intended for you.**

(For days when you need to know that it's worth the fight)

It takes a lot of hard work to align with purpose, escape the bowels of mediocrity and fully walk in your calling. But experiencing and living in the purpose that is on the other side of pain is more rewarding and fulfilling than you can imagine. It's worth the fight.

"

# As long as you're indecisive about your destiny, your future will remain uncertain.

(For days when you need to assume responsibility for the outcome of your life)

The quicker you understand that the decision is yours and that it is your responsibility to prosper, succeed and to live fulfilled, you'll move your future from the unknown into the "not yet". You have the ability to be certain about what's coming your way. But you have to take the reigns and comply with the great that's already prepared for you.

Bryan Pharr

"

**I would like to formally apologize to any and everyone that I've allowed to think that I was regular for any amount of time.**

(For days when you need to embrace your difference.)

Use this when you need to flex on the old, less authentic you. Embrace your authentic self, including your differences. Be confident. There's only one you that will ever exist. Be proud of that!

"

# Do what you love.

(For days when you're tired of doing what you hate)

As simple as it sounds, it is such a huge key to fulfillment. You were born with a purpose and have gifts that aid you in carrying that purpose out. The love that you can feel when doing a particular thing comes from the fact that the gifts you have that are designed to bring value to the people around you also feed you simultaneously. The feeling of fulfillment is felt when you are effectively using your gift(s), actively bringing value to others and receiving the joy that comes as a byproduct of your impact.

Bryan Pharr

**"**

**By the time you've spent all of your energy attempting to fix your yesterday, you will have wasted a thousand todays.**

(For days when you need to move on)

Don't allow guilt and shame to rob you of your future. You haven't lost your value and it'll take way more time to fix irreparable damage than to build something that is altogether new. You don't have to be held hostage to a past you possibly regret. Make good of your experience by learning the lessons and keep it moving. You future is waiting.

"

# If you want to keep good company, be good company.

(For days when you need to be what you need)

Attempting to put the right people around you will be a wasted effort if you aren't the right person for the people around you. Keeping good company starts with you. You may be able to get them without being good company but you can't keep them that way.

**Bryan Pharr**

"

# If you have to try to be it, you probably aren't it.

(For days when you need to get in the flow)

Everything changes when you realize that your calling or purpose doesn't require you to try to be anything. It only requires that you align yourself with who you were intended to be. It's already on the inside.

"

**Sometimes the entryway to a greater expectancy for a good outcome in your own life is the recognition of how great the grace that has been provided for your life already is.**

(For days when you need to focus on the answer)

You have two choices. Either you can focus on all of the obstacles surrounding you until they seem insurmountable or you can realize and focus on the power that you have had to overcome them the entire time until you do. You have way more than you could ever need.

Bryan Pharr

"

**A need to prove yourself to others is just a need to be approved by others wrapped in the pseudo strength of an unhealthy pride.**

(For days when you need to focus on your call)

It's a loser's game. You can never be truly confident while trying to be enough for and appease people who don't value you. Try living out your purpose. Only then will you find enough security to be unconcerned with the approval of those who don't accept you.

"

# You can't just be whatever you want to be.

(For days when you need to be real with yourself)


One of the quickest ways to throw insecurity, envy, bitterness, and a barrage of other unhealthy side effects right on top of your own head is to be unconcerned with your gifts and purpose and therefore spend the rest of your days competing with others for crowded territory. The truth is that you actually do have an option to try to be anything that pops into your head. But your purpose is the only thing that sets you apart from anyone else and places you in your own lane. The only person you're competing with within your purpose is yourself.

Bryan Pharr

"

# If service is beneath you, the dream is beyond you.

(For days when you need to step down off of your high-horse)

(My altered version of an already popular quote)…The truth about all true dreams is that there is always an intrinsic service to others woven in its fabric. Believe me when I say that a "too entitled to work" or an "unwilling to serve" mentality will lock you out from seeing a dream manifest.

"

# When you decide to win, even your enemies are blessed because they were chosen to be a part of your story.

(For days when you need to learn to appreciate the good and the bad)

In retrospect, you can probably accredit more growth and progress in your life to the pain caused by people you may consider enemies than anyone else. Their part to play has been just as vital as those who have brought peace and happiness into your life. You can't see that as coincidental. You've needed it all to continue to have every bit of greatness squeezed out of you. Both the good and the bad are collaborating to make your story one of epic proportions – if you can see it for what it is. You have to choose to use it all for your win.

Bryan Pharr

"

**People don't always reject you because they believe you're worthless. Sometimes it's because your presence costs them too much.**

(For days when you've forgotten your value)

Don't allow rejection to make you feel as if you don't have value. There probably won't be very many people who are willing to admit it, but it's often people's lack of enough capacity to be able to properly care for you that causes them to reject you.
No matter the reasoning for their rejection, you're worth more than anyone could truly ever pay for.

"

# If it's not "too good to be true", I don't want it.

(For days when you need to expect the impossible)

Don't take on someone's "too good" as your own. Don't let their declaration limit your expectation.

Bryan Pharr

"

**People have a tendency to criticize a dreamer while he or she digs the well that they will either want or need to drink from later.**

(For days when you need to count the cost of the dream)

If you aren't prepared to build without the approval or with the criticism of others present, you aren't yet prepared for the manifestation of the dream. If you aren't humble enough to become sustenance to your enemies, you aren't yet prepared for the manifestation of the dream.

"

**The world doesn't respond to you according to who you are. It responds to you according to who you're being. If you want to be treated like who you really are, you'll have to learn to be yourself.**

(For days when you need to show up as you)

You can't be disappointed when people treat you the way you've taught them based upon how you showed up. They aren't generally looking into the depths of your soul and deciding how they should treat you based upon what they see. They're responding to how you've shown up.

Bryan Pharr

"

**A true star is born when a person exchanges the pride of self-preservation for the humility needed to extend self-sacrificial service to humanity.**

(For days when you need to try being a blessing)

The entire game changes when you decide to be a blessing to others rather than always seeking a blessing from others. This life is not about self-preservation. It's about self-sacrificial love.

"

**You'll know that they're truly for you when they can celebrate the wins in your life that they don't benefit from.**

(For days when you need to take inventory of your relationships)

Be careful of people who can only celebrate you when they're directly benefiting from it – or only when they think that you're on the "same level" as them. There'll be others who can only celebrate you when they feel that they can take credit for your success.
The real ones will know that your win is always their win, even if they don't benefit from it directly.

**Bryan Pharr**

"

# Live like you're going to live forever.

(For days when you need to take a healthy risk)

Would you really be afraid to take the risks necessary to live your dream, fulfilled life if you knew that life was always on the other side of those risks?
Would you really choose to do harm to or wrong someone if you knew you'd have to see them for an eternity afterward?
Would you really treat yourself badly, dwelling on and in negative spaces if you knew you had to live with/in those results forever?
Contrary to popular belief, a fear and constant consciousness of death hinders real life rather than helps. It's an excuse and escape to those who waste their lives and a permissive agent to those who waste other's lives. Don't live that way. Live like you're going to live forever.

# Give the same patience you need.

(For days when you need more patience)

Patience can come as a result of both empathy and a genuine belief in others. When you can empathize – starting with an awareness that we all start from different places, carry different beliefs based from our backgrounds or experiences, and come to the table with a different set of circumstances – you won't become quick-tempered with people over things you believe "they should just know", mistaking what you learned from your culture and background for "common sense". Combine that awareness and empathy with a genuine belief that others can grow and change the same way you have and believe you can, and watch how patient you become with those you lead and/or influence.

Bryan Pharr

**"**

**The cost of a wasted life is much higher than that of an effective one.**

(For days when you need to make a decision)

It costs to be great. But it costs even more not to be.

"

**The path to purpose isn't discovered by attempting to seek a blessing but rather by learning to receive the need.**

(For days when you need to be an answer)

You'll always be perceived as a problem when constantly walking around with your hand out. You'll be seen as a blessing when you decide to be an answer to those around you. You become an answer when you receive the needs of others around you. Purpose will be found in your effort to be an answer.

**Bryan Pharr**

"

# If you got it your way, you wouldn't have the character to keep it.

(For days when you need to trust the process)

It isn't the dream that any of us have a problem with. It is the process that most of us have a problem with. It's the uncomfortable, challenging, tumultuous way that we have to take in order to get to our dream destination. But it's that way that produces in us the strength to capture our dream and the character to keep it. If we could choose our route or own way, the easy-peasy nature of it would leave us devoid of every attribute we needed to obtain and sustain it. Trust the process. It may be hard but it's building you so that you can build the dream.

"

# There is both a big difference and a thin line between attempting to discover your calling and trying to dodge it.

(For days when you need to make a decision)

There is certainly a time in which, at first, we may just sincerely not know what to do. But after a while, our indecisiveness is just the result of us arguing with and fighting against what we already know to do. Are you unsure or just unwilling?
**Running doesn't feel like running.**

Bryan Pharr

"

**Don't be confused. You're only having to let go of what used to ground you because you're going higher.**

(For days when you need to face your future)

It can be hard to remove yourself from the comfort and safety of what used to sustain you in one season – especially when you feel forced to for an unknown reason. But life will never stir your nest for the fun of it. There's still more potential in you that hasn't been tapped. You're going higher.

"

# Enjoying life isn't a luxury. It's an expression of sheer gratitude for life itself.

(For days when you need to get happy)

Believe it or not, you don't need a lot of material things in order to begin to enjoy life. Begin with gratitude for the opportunity that is life itself and watch how much easier it becomes to enjoy what you'll then realize is a gift.

Bryan Pharr

"

# Don't confuse what may seem like a matter of fruitfulness with what may be a matter of time.

(For days when you need to endure)

Don't give up too soon. No experienced planter expects a harvest overnight. In the same way, it's important to realize that withdrawing from your race too soon is like pulling a seed out of the ground before it has had time to produce any fruit. You'll only cut your victory short when you mistake an issue of timing for an issue of profitability. This life's journey – the journey toward your destiny – is not a speed race. It's an endurance race.
Seed…Time…Harvest

"

# At first, freedom is costly. Then it's contagious.

(For days when you need to be brave enough to be yourself)

Don't give up on being yourself now. You're freeing someone right this moment.

Bryan Pharr

"

**It isn't those who confront your complacency who should be counted as enemies. It's those who cater to your comfort who are the real threat.**

(For days when you need to cut toxic ties)

It can be easy to mistake those who lovingly challenge you to grow and progress to be enemies while assuming those who, out of their need for codependency, are more interested in you remaining comfortable where and as you are in order to remain friends. Learning to discern the difference between those who are gifted into your life to propel you to a place of peace in times of distress and those who make you content with your misery in order to maintain your current relational status will serve you well in this life.

"

# Your passion needs a place.

(For days when you need to be fruitful)

Discovering your gifts or aptitudes will not automatically push you into a purposeful life. You'll need to direct what you're passionate about toward a specific mission – one that involves servicing the world around you for its betterment. Wild passions that are not streamlined toward a specific purpose can do more damage than good. Your passion needs an intentional, productive place of expression.

Bryan Pharr

**"**

# Allow time to do its work. Often, what's cloudy will become clear with just a measure of time.

(For days when you need to be patient)

Time doesn't just "heal".
It reveals.
You won't need to jump to conclusions.
Wait until all of the facts roll in. They always do.

"

# Being "conscious" and being paranoid are not the same things. Being "woke" and being bitter are not the same things.

(For days when you need to take personal inventory of your emotions)

There is a lot of fear and jealousy under the guise of being "conscious" or "woke" going around. Anyone who has to try to "stay woke" probably isn't awake at all. It's time we began to ask what we're actually conscious of.

Bryan Pharr

"

# I grew in grace as I stretched beyond the borders of what others considered to be safe.

(For days when you need to take a chance)

You'll never know the power you hold within if you don't ever find the faith to push yourself to do more than you think you can.

"

**If you have to kill a king in order to be a king, you were never really a king.**

(For days when you need to do things the right way)

Feel free to insert "queen" where "king" currently is…

Real kings don't have to tear down anyone else in order to be king.

Bryan Pharr

"

# No amount of age-old, secondhand excuses are justification enough to die in the patterns of your past.

(For days when you need to break the pattern)

Even if the excuses that are keeping you locked out of a progressive life are "sensible" and generations old, they aren't worth wasting the potential, possibility and promise of your future. Even if you're the first to do it in your family for as far back as anyone can remember, don't be afraid to break the patterns that have held everyone back for way too long.

"

**Some of you need to fall out of love with the struggle. You're turning a pit stop into a permanent stay. You're making a momentary inconvenience your identity.**

(For days when you need to choose life)

You've overstayed your welcome in the struggle. It's time for you to prosper.

Bryan Pharr

**"**

# Betting on me is a no-brainer.

(For days when you need to believe in you)

Believe in yourself even when no one else does.

"

# Authenticity is a key to effectiveness.

(For days when you need to reach someone)

You cannot truly be effective without being authentically you. Effectiveness requires truth and transparency at its root. Without it, you may be able to dazzle and get over on a few with an innate skill and/or intelligence, but you'll lack the ability to truly and directly help anyone.

Bryan Pharr

"

# The reward for getting the work done is getting more work.

(For days when you need to find what you love)

Rather than finding work that you can tolerate for a while until you are finally elevated into a position that will "require less work"; try finding work that is fulfilling from the onset that will lead you on a path that you could travel forever if you wanted to. The misconception that promotion will lead to a less taxing experience will either lock you into a cycle of unfulfilling work or lead you to failure. The higher you go, the more responsibility you will have.

"

# Dim your light for no one.

(For days when you need to shine on)

Deciding to shine as the "star" you were always meant to be will often make you a target for those who don't like your light. But they don't have the power to dim it. Only you do. What's most important to remember when it's hard to stay encouraged through a barrage of attacks is that your light is helping plenty of others to find their own.

Bryan Pharr

**"**

# It was always you who were the key to your own fulfillment.

(For days when you need to choose life)

Fulfillment is an internal decision – not an external additive. There is no amount of approval, support, riches, friendship, etc. that you can add to your life that will do for you what one decision to lead a life of fulfillment will do. Fulfillment works from the inside, out.

"

# Real results take real faith.

(For days when you need to believe)

There is no substitute for authentic faith. Faith that does not physically work itself out cannot be considered faith at all.
The only difference between a manipulator and a manifester is that only one of them is doing the real work. If you want to truly manifest your dream(s), you'll need real faith.

**Bryan Pharr**

"

# If you be it, they won't help but see it.

(For days when you need to get real)

Most people's idea of "getting discovered" includes someone somehow pinpointing their innate, deeply hidden potential that has never been expressed. You have dreams of someone handpicking you out of a large sea of people and revealing to everyone your hidden talent – which will then lead to a long, successful career using that talent or gift through their cosign.
Rather than waiting for that moment of approval to happen and becoming more and more angry the longer it doesn't; why don't you just live out that calling or purpose on your own? If you'd just be it, they wouldn't help but see it.

"

# Truth isn't a side. It's a source

(For days when you need to be a bringer of peace)

Don't be so quick to get caught up in divisive quarrels that often attempt to force you into choosing a side. More often than not, there'll be a little truth on every side and to disregard that truth in order to pick the "right" side is always unwise. Rather than being someone who is always looking to be right, seek to be someone who is always willing to be real. Rather than looking for reasons to hate, look for reasons to love.

Bryan Pharr

"

# Celebrity is only consistency under lights.

(For days when you need to make the right impact)

Sure, not everyone has a spotlight on his or her everyday life. But everyone has an opportunity to be celebrated for what they consistently do well. Your reputation will be built upon what others get from you consistently. Why not let it be something worth celebrating? It's time for you to be famous – for all of the right reasons.

"

# How you see will be greatly shaped by who and what you hear.

(For days when you need to change who/what you're hearing)

There's enough garbage and negativity being spread to make any one of us literally hate life through the veins of much of the media we all have access to. But there's also enough positivity available to bring any one of us to life, if you're willing to search it out. You'd be surprised of the absolute life change that would happen if you began to listen to the right things.

Bryan Pharr

"

# There's a difference between bearing fruit and bearing fruit that lasts.

(For days when you need to focus on your process)

No one is exempt from the process of maturity and growth. Having any form or level of success without the character to sustain it is a curse. Even if you were born into "better" circumstances as some of you wish, that still would not exempt you from those processes. The fact that you were not born into all of the things that you wish you were may actually be your advantage for two different reasons. The first is that the journey toward what it is that you ultimately want, if traveled properly, will shape the character you need to keep what you're after. The second is that your appreciation for what you're after can often be measured by how far you had to come to get it. Don't just focus on a "winning season". Make sure you have what you need internally to make it last.

"

# Leadership is the ability to go alone.

(For days when you need to break away from the way of the crowd)

Leadership isn't determined by your ability to persuade others to go your way with your words. A manipulator can do that. Leadership will often be shown by your ability to go your own way alone and so boldly that eventually, through your proven strategies, others are convinced by your life alone. Don't be afraid to go alone – that's leading.

Bryan Pharr

"

# Your competitors don't know what they're competing with.

(For days when you need to ignore the hate)

Most of the people that are jealous of some of you are trying to feel the way you feel by attempting to amass what you have. True success sources itself from the inside and is eventually expressed on the outside. Those who become frustrated with true, outward success and try to compete with you out of their desire to "keep up" often don't realize that chasing after what you own won't make them feel how you feel. Happiness is an inside job.

# Guilt causes separation.

(For days when you need to release the guilt)

Unwarranted guilt is not only toxic because of its depressive qualities but also because of its need for isolation. Guilt will have you avoiding situations and people for no reason at all, especially after coupled with its close partner shame. Some of you are holding yourself responsible for things that aren't your fault. Move on.

Bryan Pharr

**"**

# Stop asking, "who's going to…?", and start asking, "how can I…?".

(For days when you need to take responsibility)

When looking at all of "what's wrong" in the world, you may be tempted to shift responsibility to everyone other than you for how things will change. News flash – things won't change without you. Unless you embrace being a part of the change, things cannot fully be better around you.

# They'll treat you how you see you.

(For days when you need to set a standard)

It's not what others believe about you that will ultimately determine how they treat you. It's how you see and feel about yourself that will be the determinate factors. You set the standard for what is allowed in your life. Not everyone automatically knows how they should treat you. Teach them. And those who don't have the capacity for what you need will leave. You won't be able to get any better treatment from others than you give to yourself.

Bryan Pharr

"

# What you can't know in the wait, you'll learn on the way.

(For days when you need to be brave)

Purpose isn't often found in stillness but rather in service and in stewardship. Waiting to discover who you are and/or why you're here before you move around in life will keep you stagnant and unproductive. You'll discover along the way. You'll be surprised at the revelation that can come to you as you go about living normal life.

"

# Don't kill your friends.

(For days when you need to be a real friend)

Love can show itself in many ways, but standing by and allowing your "friends" to harm themselves in the form of self-destructive behavior all in the name of "letting them do what makes them happy", is not one of them. Real friends hold their friends accountable. Real friends tell their friends the truth.

Bryan Pharr

"

# The quickest way to be blessed is to become a blessing.

(For days when you need to break out of "not enough")

Rather than chasing provision, aim to be a provider. When you seek to give rather than only to get, you start cycles of blessing in your life. Every seed planted returns multiplied times what it was sown. Become a giver.

"

# Don't be afraid to let your past lead you.

(For days when you need to take inventory)

"Hindsight is 20/20". You can learn a lot from taking your past decisions and their direct consequences into account. You'll often learn what you should not do again. And you'll also learn what you should do more of. You'll be surprised by the amount of direction and number of secrets about your own life that are revealed in the breadcrumbs of the patterned actions within your journey thus far.

Bryan Pharr

"

# No one is ever too full of kindness.

(For days when you need to share what you have)

Don't ever feel as if someone "probably doesn't need" the loving kindness you want to show them in the form of a word of encouragement, appreciation, etc. Most of the time, even those who seem to be adored by many – especially the "strong ones" among us – are often more deficient of those kind words and actions than we may imagine. That's because many assume they probably already have enough. Regardless of who it is, don't shy away from gifting others with your kindness. It may change someone's entire day – or even life!

"

# Peace comes from an unwavering trust that the process has already been provided for.

(For days when you need peace)

Before living too long, you should begin to recognize that every obstacle or hard time that has presented itself in your past has also been a situation that you have had the provision and power to make it through thus far. Sometimes, the quickest way for you to embrace peace in the middle of what may seem like an unfavorable circumstance you are currently experiencing, is to realize that, just like in times past, this process has already been provided for. You've made it through before. You'll do it again.

Bryan Pharr

"

# Don't permit yourself to do wrong just because you see wrong around you.

(For days when you need to see the good)

It can almost seem logical to cut corners, lie, cheat, steal and to do what's wrong in general if you justify yourself doing so because of "the state of the world". Don't just focus on the negative things you see around you. Find the positive around you that is more present than you may even currently believe. It'll constantly remind you of your opportunity and power to be the change that the rest of the world needs to see.

"

# You'll always win at being you.

(For days when you need to focus)

Don't allow yourself to feel disqualified or to get discouraged because you can't seem to outrun or keep up with some of the other runners in this "race" we call life. The truth is that you weren't meant to compete with anyone else in the first place. Your job is to run your own race, becoming the best you that you can. This means that you will have to stay focused on your own lane long enough to learn how to run it well. It's not that you won't or can't be inspired by other runners along the way. But there's a huge difference between getting inspired and getting intimidated. You can't beat others at their race. But you can always win at yours.

Bryan Pharr

"

# True love is expressed for yourself and others when you learn to forgive without needing to find a reason to.

(For days when you need to forgive)

If you use a measurement of your pain and the severity of an offense as a means of figuring out whether or not you should forgive someone, you probably never will. Forgiveness is a gift that you give both to yourself and to an offender. It cannot be earned and should be given, even when undeserved. Forgiveness is the key to your freedom from a bitterness that might otherwise lock out future joys that would enter into your life.

"

# You can never be given what you haven't made room for.

(For days when you need to let go)

Old and new can never truly coexist. Seasons of "transition" are ones in which the old is being filtered away from your life so that you can embrace something altogether new – a new you, a new life, a new relationship, a new season, a new opportunity, a new responsibility, a new purpose or assignment – a new thing that will cost you something old. Even a new mindset will require you to rid yourself of an old mindset. Learning to let go in these seasons is prime and is what will allow you to step into what's next. Without the ability to let go of the old, you cannot enter into the new.

Bryan Pharr

"

# Good times conceal.
# Bad times reveal.

(For days when you need to appreciate it all)

We often take for granted the times when it seems everything is going wrong in our lives. They carry just as much purpose as any of the times that would normally be labeled "good". They reveal to us where our trust is and how strong our internal foundations are. They also reveal to us the hearts of those who are around us many times. Those that gravitate to you when things seem to be going great in your life aren't always apt to stick around when things don't seem favorable for you. There are others that you will find were with you for the long run. Cherish the "bad times" just as well as the good.

> **A true blessing isn't locational. It's internal. A true blessing isn't circumstantial. It's eternal.**

(For days when you need to be reminded of who you are)

Everything changes when you realize that you are the blessing. This is not to say that there aren't physical locations or places where you will be able to thrive and others where you may only be able to survive. Rather, it should be your aim to be a blessing no matter where you are – because that is what you are. Though every place may not be for you, you can decide to be for the wellbeing of every place you find yourself. You can choose to be blessed no matter the circumstance.

Bryan Pharr

"

**Deadweight is the enemy of altitude and a doubled vision is the enemy to progression. Preparation is a prerequisite to every climb.**

(For days when you need to prepare)

When preparing to make a climb, it is a necessity to loose dead wait and to gain focus. You'll need every advantage available to make it where you're going.

"

# Your value is not in what you lost.

(For days when you need to move on)

It can be hard not to feel as if you've lost a part of your worth when dealing with great loss in your life – especially large career losses or close relationships. But when going through seasons of refinement in your life, no matter how great the loss is, it is never your value that is cut away. As a matter of fact, refinement cuts everything away except what is valuable.

Bryan Pharr

**"**

# You don't need everyone on your side. You just need the right one.

(For days when you need to wait for the right one)

Don't concern yourself with winning everyone over to be a part of the dream you have for your own life. We sometimes overestimate what we'll need to see the dream manifest. We feel as if we need everyone when in all actuality we only need the right one(s). The entire world can be against you but with the right partnership, nothing can stop you!

"

# All of your true opportunities will be shaped just like you.

(For days when you need to make a decision)

Believe it or not, every opportunity in life that is truly yours will fit you perfectly and will feel as if it was designed and waiting just for you. "Good" opportunities aren't always good for you. You'll know the right ones when you see them. Choose fit over funds.

Bryan Pharr

"

**I'm glad to know that you've realized you're loved. Now it's time to start believing that you're lovable.**

(For days when you need to up your expectations)

Try confessing this: People are fighting to be my friend.

You aren't just loved. You're lovable.

"

**The distance between where you are and the life you dream of living is a measure of faith.**

(For days when you need to take inventory)

The dream doesn't just come about haphazardly. What you need to ask yourself is if you have enough unwavering belief and assurance to bring that dream from your imagination or from the invisible into fruition. If you don't, feed yourself with the things that will grow your faith.

**Bryan Pharr**

"

# You're loved, accepted and free.

(For days when you need to overcome)

When you begin to understand, realize and accept these truths, the inward lies that sought to keep you bound will begin to dissipate. You're loved, accepted and free – and it's not your fault.

"

# Be sure that's a circle you're a part of and not a cult.

(For days when you need to be real)

You ever had to hold back from being yourself or from showing love to a particular person or group because your circle doesn't approve? You ever had to stop associating with good people and taking advice or listening to them for fear of being kicked out of your circle? Ever felt like you don't have what it takes to accomplish anything outside of your circle?...
That's not a circle. That's a cult. Control is the difference.

Bryan Pharr

"

# As long as you're standing on the shore of convenience, you'll never know the depth, power, effect and reach of real love.

(For days when you need to take a real chance)

So many of our relational lives only involve a bunch of business transactions disguised as relationships. We date and relate for a "come-up" and once the relationship introduces an inconvenience or doesn't look like our business plan anymore, we bail out. Love is the catalyst for a truly fruitful relationship.

"

**It's the imperfections, inconsistencies, inconveniences and hard times we face that prove our love – not the good times.**

(For days when you need to stay in the fight)

Love cannot be labeled unconditional until it has been tried in the fires of hard times. You'll never know whether true love exists within a relationship until you've had to battle through tough times, whether created by an external event or through one another.

**Bryan Pharr**

"

# Your purpose is realized, not reached. It is discovered, not decided.

(For days when you need to be yourself)

Your purpose is so woven into your being that you probably often think nothing of it. We sometimes look right over it in an attempt to find "something more spectacular". Your gifts are so natural to you that it's quite possible that you're taking them for granted right this moment. You may not be using them to their focused potential or in the way that you should but they're already there. Life becomes way more fulfilling once you realize the gifts that are latent and use them for the betterment of the world around you. You only trouble yourselves and others the most when attempting to force yourself against your own innate design.

"

**Frustration is often a gift given to align or realign someone with a fruitful existence.**

(For days when you need to be reminded of who you are)

Frustration is often a side effect of a lack of fruitfulness. You don't have to despise frustration. It's only an indicator. If you learn to see it as such, you'll know its potential to spark your desire for a more fruitful state of being.

Bryan Pharr

**"**

# Chasing provision will often leave you empty-handed. Pursue the vision and provision will find you.

(For days when you need to change your focus)

Most people have been trained to make a continued and popular mistake – chase money. After doing so, most end up with way less than they intended to have and also have to put themselves in unfulfilling positions and on unfulfilling paths. It's a distraction.
Pursue purpose instead. Fulfillment and provision have already been provided on the path of purpose.

Wisdom – For Days

"

# Everything you need to thrive is on the inside.

(For days when you need to believe in you)

One of the most common traps set for those of you who lack self-belief is the trap of codependence. There are people everywhere who are ready to affirm and take advantage of the idea that you aren't good enough to find success on your own. But the truth is really that you have all you could ever need to be the best you possible – inside. It isn't that you cannot learn from or benefit from collaboration or partnership with others. We are better together. But to allow anyone to make you or help you believe that you are nothing or nobody without them is to make the drastic mistake of needing someone else to make you what you could be. This will lead you into a limited, unfulfilling existence.

Bryan Pharr

"

# You cannot stand in victory with the one you wouldn't stand with in the fight.

(For days when you need to "man-up")

You should not expect to benefit from the victory of a fight you were not willing to take part in – especially when you were given an opportunity to. That type of entitlement will keep you with the poorest of the poor.

"

# You don't need permission for what has already been purposed.

(For days when you need to step out)

Your purpose is your duty. To wait for permission to live out your purpose would also be to neglect the responsibility you have to ensure that it is walked out.

Bryan Pharr

"

# It's hard to talk to who you've been talking about.

(For days when you need to face the truth)

Sometimes the distance you feel being created between yourself and someone else is signification of their change of mind concerning how they see you. Once expressed to another person who shares their same viewpoint, it becomes increasingly hard for them to put on the mask of their old viewpoint in order to relate to you the same. In other words, rather than continually submitting themselves to the uncomfortable position of having to pretend that they don't view you negatively, they'll distance themself from you. If you suspect this to be the case with someone you know, always be sure that what you're suspecting is the actual reality – but once you discover the truth; accept it for what it is. Don't force someone to do what they don't want.

"

# Only quality seeds produce quality harvests.

(For days when you need to make an adjustment)

Are you frustrated because of the company, clientele or conclusions that seem to just be attracted to you? You may need to "plant" better quality "seeds" in your life. What is coming back to you is always a direct indication of what you're putting out. If you want to produce high-quality results in your life, do high-quality work.

Bryan Pharr

"

# You don't need a new land. You need a new level.

(For days when you need to level up)

There is no substitute for taking the necessary chances required to play on the next level when that time comes in your life. Most of you who are bored to death and exhausted from trying to pull everyone up around you, who you've already outgrown years ago, don't actually need to up and move locations in order to be fulfilled as you may assume. Some of you are in the right place but are playing the wrong position. You need a new goal. You need a new circle. You need a new challenge. You need a new fight. You need a new level of responsibility that you won't find on the level you've been playing on for so long. If you moved away just to stay and play on the same level, you still wouldn't be happy. Level up.

"

# If there was a way in, there is a way out.

(For days when you need to receive freedom)

You are not where you are for "no reason". When we close our eyes to how we've either created or allowed our current circumstances, we chain ourselves to the misery of life happening to us and not for us. Taking responsibility for the current reality in your life is also acceptance of the freedom to change your reality should you choose to. You aren't stuck. You only need to realize your power to improve all that is ailing you.

Bryan Pharr

"

# Your need to fit in is preventing you from standing out.

(For days when you need to be yourself)

There are two types of compromise that will result in an unfulfilling life. One type involves cloaking yourself in the opinions, beliefs and trends of the crowds around you in order to fit in with them. The second type involves attempting to "hide in plain sight" in order to avoid any interaction with the crowds knowing that you may be criticized for your difference. Both forms are detrimental to your fulfillment and should not be embraced as acceptable lifestyles.

Wisdom – For Days

"

# You don't need to know every step in order to go every step.

(For days when you need to up your faith)

Living out your dream is comparable to driving down a road that is covered in thick fog. If you've ever had this experience, you'll know that you're only able to see a few feet in front of you at a time, even with the assistance of headlights. Every journey to the dream requires faith – meaning that you have to hold on to the belief of an expected end although you aren't able to see every step you're going to have to take. You can make it if you have the faith to go the distance.

CCLI

Bryan Pharr

"

# Empathy is the result of understanding.

(For days when you need to be patient)

It is important to look beneath the surface of what is often destructive or, at the least, annoying behavior from others. What getting to the root of the behavior does is allows you to realize that the actions are only symptoms and not the sickness. This, in the end, will allow you to become less judgmental, more patient and even provide the freedom to forgive. Empathy is not an excuse to allow destructive behavior to run rampant but rather a lens that will aid you in becoming a help to someone's process.

"

# You are not awaiting your destiny. Your destiny is awaiting your change.

(For days when you need to be ok with change)

Don't allow anyone to discourage, discount or discredit your change. It is a necessity for you to become.
In the same way that the sky, wind and air combine to be a prepared place for the caterpillar once it has gone through its transformation, your destiny is the prepared place that is awaiting your transformation. You aren't waiting on it. It's already prepared and waiting on you.

Bryan Pharr

"

# No one can stop the harvest from the seeds you dared to plant and water.

(For days when you need to believe)

A true enemies' only tactic is to get you so full of doubt and unbelief that you never even take the first step – or to get you to quit during the process due to a growing unbelief along the way. A true enemy knows that if you would dare to take a chance on that dream and endure the process to see it through, he or she could not stop the harvest that would come as a result of your effort. If your enemy believes so strongly in your potential and destiny that they would spend time and effort to prevent you from ever seeing it, maybe you should believe in it also.

"

# What you're graced with is more powerful than what you're faced with.

(For days when you need to see it differently)

When what you're facing seems insurmountable, remember that there is more working for you than against you. When you see what you have as greater than what you need, you'll be able to overcome every obstacle that comes your way on the way to your destiny.

Bryan Pharr

**"**

# Your self-image will either be determined by what they say or by what you know.

(For days when you need to take control)

If you would dare go through the long, grueling but rewarding process of getting to know yourself, you could take the control of your self-image into your own hands. Without it, you will be continually tossed between differing opinions formed by those who will attempt to define you from their limited perspective. If you would endure that process, you could stand on not just who you think you are but who you know yourself to be.

"

# A commitment with options isn't a commitment at all.

(For days when you need to go all in)

Every dream deserves a full commitment. It deserves that you throw yourself at it fully, being fully decided having relieved yourself of all other options. No dream can manifest through inconsistent efforts.

Bryan Pharr

"

# Vision puts all of the good days in front of you.

(For days when you need to let go)

Are you using all of your time obsessing over the "good ol' days" of your past or are you using your imagination to envision your best days that have yet to come? A lack of vision will leave you to the hopeless attempts of trying to relive days that have long past and will never return. Vision is the key to freeing you from both the joys and the pains of your past.

"

## Extraordinary is a choice.

(For days when you need to be willing)

We all have the ability to explore and express the potential for extraordinary that is latent within every fiber of our being. But you'll need the desire and willingness to step beyond the ordinary bounds that much of the world lives behind. Greatness is an agreement and partnership between you and the potential you have always had that is simply waiting to be expressed.

Bryan Pharr

"

# True life will not force itself upon anyone.

(For days when you need to give in)

The joys and the pleasures of true life are readily waiting to rush into the life of the one who is willing to open himself or herself up to it. This type of fulfilling existence does not resist us. Therefore, anyone who is not experiencing it is only resisting it. Love, prosperity, abundance, joy, happiness and the many other characteristics of a "good life" that anyone would love to experience all must be embraced. Believing and receiving is the way.

"

# Yesterday's victory can fuel your faith within todays struggle.

(For days when you need to be fearless)

Simply remembering how much you have already overcome can replace the fear and anxiety that is trying to be formed through your current struggle with faith. Although the battle may be different, after a while, we should be able to conclude that the same grace we had that brought us through previous battles is present with us today and will bring us through what we're facing again. Replacing that fear and anxiety with faith makes way for enjoyment and hopeful expectation to enter your fighting days until your victory is won.

**Bryan Pharr**

"

# Stop trying and start trusting.

(For days when you need to trust the process)

"Where we think we should be by now", "what we feel like we shouldn't have to go through" and "who we think we should be with" are all examples of ideas that often get in the way of the natural and necessary progression of life that prepares us for a life beyond our wildest dreams. Many times, the shortcuts we attempt to find and implement into our lives that are designed to help us to compete with our peers also cut short our destinies, growth, progress and maturity. If you'd just stop trying things your way and trust the process, you'd find that what you had in mind for your life while competing with your friends was way less satisfying and way less fulfilling than the life that was intended for you the entire time.

"

# You won't manifest any dream by only doing what you want. You'll have to grow into doing what it takes.

(For days when you need to grow up)

There's a certain amount of selflessness that is required to truly be great and make an impact on the world around you. You'll need to put the needs of others above your own at times, take responsibility, sacrifice and do things that you may not prefer doing in the moment. Greatness requires maturity, discipline and a willingness to go the extra mile. If you only do what you like or feel like doing, you will fall dramatically short of an excellent life. Do what it takes.

**Bryan Pharr**

"

# Re-write your story.

(For days when you need to change how you see it)

Our lives often suffer from the way we label certain events that don't feel the best while we're experiencing them. Some of you need to re-label what you've called rejection as direction or protection. You need to re-label what you've named failure as lessons, wisdom and knowledge disguised as disappointment. You need to re-label what you've described as "tests and trials" as agents to build your strength. When you re-label what are often labeled as tragic events, you began to see that they were all set-ups and preparation for greatness to invade your life.

"

**Just know before anything extraordinary happens that I thought the world of myself before the world even knew to think of me.**

(For days when you need to believe in yourself)

You believe – then they believe.

Bryan Pharr

"

# It's time to stop stating the facts and to start facing the facts.

(For days when you need to cut the excuses)

Honesty should have an expiration date. At some point, it should no longer be acceptable to use the power of honesty about where you are, where you're from, who violated you along the way, how you feel and how you're behaving in order to form excuses for why you can't become the best version of you. It may be true that you've gone through a lot. But what is also true is that you possess the power necessary to change the trajectory of your life and rise to your highest self.

"

## Only the wise have come to count even their enemies as friends of their destiny.

(For days when you need to change how you see it)

Sometimes a good enemy is the only push you need to make it to your destiny. Wisdom allows you to recognize that enemy as a vessel and instrument for you rather than against you in the grand scheme of things. Be thankful for the push of an enemy.

Bryan Pharr

"

# You're dope…and it's not your fault.

(For days when you need to be grateful)

Without having accomplished a thing, you can be grateful for the privilege it is to be born a human. The thought of the power and potential that is latent within every fiber of your being is enough to start every morning on a high. The powers to reason, dream, create, manifest and build are all accessible in every moment. The potential for a greatness that outlasts your own lifespan is in every one of us. The ability to change someone's day or even their life for the better is a privilege of human existence. Make no mistake – being dope is only agreeing with who you were created and are graced to be.

"

# Regret is the reward for continually burying the voice of potential in your life.

(For days when you need to make a choice)

It's not as hard as it should be to ignore the inner voice that is continuously urging you to live a higher existence – to expect more, to do more and to live better. That voice of potential, whether speaking up from the inside or through an outside vessel, is the voice that is always offering a choice, forcing you to decide how your life's story will ultimately read.

Bryan Pharr

"

# Work, even when the results are unseen.

(For days when you need to trust the process)

Whether you realize it or not, your working is not in vain. Your seeds of effort are doing more for you than you know. It can be easy to get discouraged by a lack of obvious results – especially when you've been working hard toward an expected end that you want to actually see manifest. But just know that, even when the results aren't obvious, all of your effort, diligence, endurance, responsibility, faith, courage, goodness and more are all working on your behalf, even when you stop and more than you can see. There are plenty who are being affected positively that you are unaware of. Every seed grows below the ground first – unseen and undetected before it can become in the light.

"

**The wisdom, knowledge and understanding that you've gained through your experiences, both good and bad, are the bricks you are meant to lay to help someone else cross over.**

(For days when you need to lend a helping hand)

Be a bridge. Don't just use what you've learned through your experiences to be a better person and keep the information to yourself. You can use what you've learned to help someone who is going through what you've gone through. Just for them to know that you have already come through what they may feel like is currently killing them is often times enough for them to make it through themselves.

Bryan Pharr

"

# A lack of control will make anxiety your copilot.

(For days when you need to turn fear into faith)

Anxiety is a fear that is formed when projecting danger, misfortune or a negative outcome on your future in your mind. Although a symptom of having anxiety can be to become overly controlling, anxiety often starts from a lack of control. If you were to ever sit in the back seat of any non-autonomously-driving car while it was in drive with a brick on the gas pedal and no one steering, you'd have loads of anxiety. Rightfully taking responsibility and control of the areas of your life that you have just left to chance and have mismanaged will offset the anxiety that comes as a byproduct of your neglect. Get a positive vision for your life and intentionally steer in the direction of that outcome.

"

# Fulfillment is in the finish.

(For days when you need to press on)

If you keep starting and stopping, never completing any tasks or assignments you begin; you can never feel the joys of fulfillment. It can be challenging to stay at it during the mundane, annoying, exhausting, difficult moments that are a part of every great outcome. But you'll need to press through if you ever hope to see a dream realized or manifested.

Bryan Pharr

"

# Don't forsake your best for the comfort within your mess.

(For days when you need to move on)

It isn't the misery within the spaces we shouldn't be that keeps us there. It is the comfort and familiarity within those places that we often trade the greatness of our potential for. It is never worth it. Get a vision that is so big and so compelling that you are willing to escape your comfort zone to grab hold of it. A miserable life with a little comfort will never come close to comparing to a fulfilled one.

"

# Faith is a matter of being willing enough and humble enough to receive what you don't deserve.

(For days when you need to believe anyway)

The last thing any one of us should place our faith in is our being "perfect enough" to be blessed. There's no such thing. Faith is often exemplified in the person who is able to believe in their destiny enough to pursue it despite their faults.

**Bryan Pharr**

"

# The key to your next is within what you have left.

(For days when you need to value what you have)

Don't believe any voice that says you aren't where you want to be because of something you don't have. The key to getting where you want to go is always wrapped in the potential of what you already have. You haven't come close to exhausting what's possible if you'd put what you have to work. Rather than focusing on what you don't have, focus on making the most of what is currently in your possession.

"

# Leadership is the ability to go first.

(For days when you need to be real)

If you always need permission, affirmation, belief, encouragement and understanding from others around you before you can lead, you aren't fit for leadership. Leadership is self-affirming, self-permitting, self-believing and self-pushing. If you can't go, do or be without another person's consent you're a follower and need to be admittedly.

Bryan Pharr

**"**

# The heights you can experience will always coincide with the lows you can handle.

(For days when you need to face the facts)

Make no mistake about it – there is a cost for success of a high magnitude. The cost is as great as the reward. If you do not have a tolerance for pain that can handle the jealousy, hatred, competition and criticism that will come as a result of any rise or promotion, it would be best that you remain in and enjoy the place that you are. You shouldn't be discontented concerning where you are if you are unwilling to pay the cost for where you believe you want to be.

"

# Stop looking for a way out and start looking for a way up.

(For days when you need to embrace patience)

Every shortcut you attempt to take on your journey toward the dream or toward success will result in a shortage of what you'll need to sustain what you gain. If you want your success to be long lasting, embrace every bit of pain, struggle and hard work it takes to endure the process the right way. You won't regret it in the end. Skipped steps mean skipped lessons. Don't look for a way out of the process. Work your way up.

Bryan Pharr

**"**

# Stop waiting on the world to shine a light on you. Be the light the world needs to shine.

(For days when you need to find your shine)

A true star shines on its own and the world comes to watch.

"

# Potential won't open doors. Practice will.

(For days when you need to get to work)

There are some of you who are bold and naïve enough to look for and request opportunities based off of some hidden potential that you feel will work itself out once you receive that opportunity. Unless the person who is giving the opportunity is only looking to take advantage of you or use you, you won't be able to shortcut your way into any doors of opportunity really worth having. Real opportunities will only come by way of what you've already proven yourself to be by putting your aptitudes to work. Putting your innate abilities into practice is what will bring opportunities to you. You won't have to go looking for an open door that way. They'll open themselves.

Bryan Pharr

"

**For all of the chatter I've heard about people "selling their souls" for money or fame; I've seen people sell out for a lot less.**

(For days when you need to make a move)

It can be easy to throw verbal stones at someone who is "rich and famous", calling them a sellout for the way you've either heard or believe they have attained their status. But choosing to trade your calling or dream for any career path – even one that is multiplied times less lucrative – is committing the same "sin". Don't be too quick to judge and become self-righteous concerning those in the light who may be wronging themselves in the same way that you currently are. No matter what your social and economic statuses are, if you aren't living a fulfilled life, you need to prioritize what's most important – you.

"

# Knowledge reveals options where there were none.

(For days when you need to grow)

Sometimes the only barrier between where you are and where you want to be is what you don't know. This is why it is important to continue to learn and grow in experience, knowledge and understanding. The times in your life that you feel stuck and hopeless will often come to an end with a piece of information that will show you a way out where you thought there was none. You have way more choices in life than you may realize – concerning your health, finances, career and many other things that are important to you. Those options reveal themselves the more you are willing to be open to new ideas and principles that will propel you in the direction you ultimately dream of going.

**Bryan Pharr**

"

# They'll often love the picture but hate the process.

(For days when you need to move on)

Ideas sound great while you're painting a picture to others of what you ultimately want to accomplish. There will even be others who will celebrate the potential they see in you and the outcome they feel is possible for your life. But living out that potential can normally bring a different reaction out of those same people. It's often the people who love your potential who later learn to hate your process because of the fact that it usually requires that you outgrow them – especially those who do not grow with you during your process or are not destined to walk with you into your potential. Seek understanding during the process so that you do not hold on to "what used to be" too long and hinder your progress.

"

**Trying to build your worth is like a diamond trying to be something else in order to be valuable.**

(For days when you need to know your value)

Your worth is realized, not built.

**Bryan Pharr**

"

# Who you're being will always determine what you can have.

(For days when you need to change your behavior)

You'll have to be it before you can see it. Victories only come to those who are victorious. Wealth only comes to those who are wealthy. Health only manifests in those who are healthy. This is why your behavior is such an important factor to your success. Those who want a certain outcome behave like it before it even shows up physically in their life.
Be.
Have.
Behave(ior)

"

**Manipulation starts with expecting or needing something you won't just ask for. It ends with attempting to turn others into what you need without their consent or them even deciding whether they can or want to be it.**

(For days when you need to be straight up)

If you need something, just ask. People have the freedom to choose whether or not they can or want to give you what you need. Trying to find ways to force them to give you what you need when they haven't consented to – no matter the need – is manipulation. If no one answers your need willingly after you've asked, pray and take the responsibility upon yourself to do what needs to be done.

Bryan Pharr

"

# People don't die from a lack of knowledge. They die from their lack of knowledge.

(For days when you need to seek an answer)

Want to know the secret to living a fulfilled life? Here it is: there is no secret. Just like all of the wisdom keys that are laid out plainly in this book for all to see, every secret is laid out on full display daily for humanity to see. Whether through nature, books like this one, other humans or the "endless" amount of information that can be found on the internet, the truth you need to live your greatest life is readily available at a moment's decision. If you are humble enough to search it out and filter through the bad information, you'll find it. You can even tap the invisible with a simple acknowledgement and ask for pure truth straight from the source.

"

# Codependency turns what should only be an option into an obligation.

(For days when you need rely on you)

A lack of options is sometimes the sign of codependence. It shows that you rely too heavily on people, things or institutions around you. Every additive in life should be considered an option in order to maintain a healthy relationship with that additive. For instance, higher education is an option for learning but not always a necessity. If you had to, you could learn on your own the very things that are taught there. When you get to the point of not being able to live, thrive or succeed without a particular person, thing, or institution, you have allowed codependence to take over. Having a healthy reliance on ourselves is what brings health and balance to our relationships with the outside world. We all need help at times but codependence will always send the wrong help.

Bryan Pharr

**"**

# A positive outlook won't always change what you experience in life. But it will always change how you experience life.

(For days when you need to change how you see it)

A positive person and a pessimistic person could both be standing outside on the same day, in the same place, at the same time, in the same weather, underneath the same sun. One would describe their experience as "hellish". The other would describe the same experience as "heavenly". You may not be able to always change what you're experiencing, but the way you see it will always affect how you are experiencing it. Take on the positive outlook.

"

# What you can truly hear or understand will always be relevant to where you are.

(For days when you need to be patient)

It can be hard to listen to and understand a parent who, in essence, is speaking to you from the future and from their experience when you've only been alive for so long. This is because you don't yet have enough experience and context many times to even begin to really know what they are talking about. There is a gap in-between where you are in life and where they are. At the time, the information will seem almost irrelevant and inapplicable. You need to know that much of what seems irrelevant will become relevant the closer you get to where they are. You won't need it all, but you'll need a good bit of it. This principle can be applied in reverse or anywhere there is a gap in communication between two people or more.

**Bryan Pharr**

"

# The things that you left behind are still behind you for a reason.

(For days when you need to stay focused)

After a while, progress and new experiences can make you forget why you moved on from stagnant situations in your past in the first place. If you aren't careful, you'll find yourself retracing your steps, going back with a hopeful expectancy that things have changed and becoming disappointed all over again because of the false hope you carried with you. You saw it right the first time. It is what it is. They are who they are. There is a reason they're still there. Don't look back.

Wisdom – For Days

"

# Don't overestimate your strength. Some things are too heavy to fly with.

(For days when you need to let go)

Be carful about playing what you may think is a "savior" role. Some of you are constantly asking yourselves why it seems as if you can't get things to take off when you're trying with all of your might to get them in the air. The truth is that you really are exerting enough energy to get things going. But the problem is all of the things and people you're trying to carry with you. I know you want to save everyone by taking them with you, but if they aren't carrying their own weight, they can't go. You aren't built to force anyone in the air with you. They have to fly for themselves just as you do – if they want to.

Bryan Pharr

"

# Everyone loves your potential until it's pointed in their direction.

(For days when you need to be more aware)

There will be a lot of people who love the idea of who you could be as long as they can use it to their advantage. These same people will try to assassinate you for the same potential they see in you if they don't have control over it and begin viewing you as competition. The same potential and gifts or aptitudes that will inspire some will threaten others. It's best to be in places where you aren't just being used and can generally call those who work with you collaboratively friends. Don't be afraid to meet your potential but be aware of the actions and intent of everyone around you. Those who are truly for you won't need to benefit from you in order to support you.

"

# Don't find your fit. Find your purpose.

(For days when you need to be ok with being different)

Living in alignment with your given purpose and intention in this world is not about fitting in. As a matter of fact, living out your purpose is what will set you apart from everyone else. It is a unique call that isn't shared with anyone else on this planet. Fitting in is how you make yourself into a cheap imitation of someone else. Being willing to stand out and walk in your individual purpose is what will bring the most value from your life and fulfillment to your life.

**Bryan Pharr**

"

# You will always have to endure suffering where you don't implement systems.

(For days when you need to better care for what you have)

Systems are what you use to manage and maintain a particular thing. If you are suffering in your health, I can guarantee that you don't and have not had a system in place that would maintain your health – one that consists of scheduled and obligatory healthy diet and exercise. If you are suffering in your finances, I can guarantee that you have not implemented any systems for the income and maintenance of your money. If you are suffering in your relationships – especially the really meaningful ones – I can guarantee you have not implemented any systems to maintain them. All you need is a system.

"

# Only free men can free men.

(For days when you need to go first)

For all of you who feel as if you can help someone out of a situation you're bound to: don't fool yourself. You'll need to be free before you can free anyone else. You won't know the way to freedom until you've freed yourself. On the flip side, if anyone offers you freedom and are bound themself – run.

Bryan Pharr

"

# An anyhow attitude can take you anywhere you want to go.

(For days when you need to endure)

Locked or closed "doors" or opportunities won't stop an anyhow attitude. "Noes" or rejection can't stop an anyhow attitude. This type of endurance is what leads you to find a way where there is none. You'll create a lane if all the others are closed. It's not about forcing your way through other people to your destiny. It's about fighting your way to your destiny even if you have to go alone. It's less about being willing to do absolutely anything and more about being willing to press on to your expected end even though things don't always go the way you hoped.

"

# When you know you're a king/queen, doing the work of a peasant won't bother you.

(For days when you need to do the work)

Needing to prove your royalty by treating others like crap and refusing to do anything that feels "beneath you" is a manifestation of pride and low self-esteem. A true king or queen who knows who they are has enough humility to serve and to be serviced. Neither is beneath them. When you know who you are and are secure, you can do what others won't and not feel any less than royalty. True royalty comes from the inside.

**Bryan Pharr**

"

**You're not my project.
You're my partner.
You're not my realist.
You're my rider.
You're not my assistant.
You're my assignment.
This isn't a convenience.
It's a covenant.**

(For days when you need to be reminded of what marriage is all about)

Don't "fix" them. Support them.
Don't tear down their dreams. Build them up and be with him or her for the ride.
Don't always look to be helped. Be the first to help.
Don't bail out on them when things get rough. Stay in the fight – focused and committed.

CCC

"

# Don't waste time "sparing feelings". Live honestly.

(For days when you need to stand up)

Don't let your truth be held hostage by their feelings. What you believe you're doing "for them" is only hurting you. And the longer you hold back the truth; you're, in all actuality, only hurting more and more people. I know you believe that hiding and not fully living honestly is sparing others from pain, but living dishonestly is what will eventually cause the most pain. Lies can only cover up the truth for so long. You aren't responsible for anyone's immaturity, ignorance or/and insecurities that may not allow them to handle your truth. Live honestly and be willing to receive the consequences of doing so.

Bryan Pharr

"

# Don't idolize; imitate.

(For days when you need to join the fight)

The world needs more heroes. You can never be one of them while doubting your own capability to do what the heroes of our day are doing. The greatest leaders give others permission to be as great as them and better. They only seek to be the first of many. Don't idolize these heroes, waiting around for them to solve everyone's problems – including yours. Join in the fight! Take responsibility for the problems in the world around you and imitate their heroic ways. You can be a hero too – in your own way.

Wisdom – For Days

"

# You don't have an output problem. You have an input problem.

(For days when you need to invest in you)

If you're battling with not having enough to give, sometimes the simple answer is to get more. If you don't have enough energy to give throughout the day, you may not be getting enough sleep or rest and nourishment for you body. If you don't have enough money to give, you probably just need to find a way to earn or get more money. If you don't have any love to give, you probably haven't received love. The root cause isn't your ability to output. It's you willingness to input.

Bryan Pharr

"

# Don't allow an old victory to cut you off from new victories ahead.

(For days when you need to kill the high horse)

Getting "drunk" off of your last win is a sure way to cut your potential short and may even lead to new failure. This isn't a shot against celebrating – but celebrating too long, getting high off your success, becoming prideful and slowing your progress will lead to your downfall. This is often the result of a competitor's mindset. You shouldn't be in anything to compete. You should only be out to dominate – which also means you should really only be competing with yourself. There are more victories to be won. But you have to be progressing for the right reasons.

"

# False hope keeps you in a cycle of non-progressive movement.

(For days when you need to let go)

Hope is what will keep your feet moving even when things look dark or grim. Progression is what necessitates you letting go of what isn't working so that you can actually move forward.
False hope is what keeps you going but at the same time will not allow you to let go of what isn't working. Movement does not equal progression. Let go.

Bryan Pharr

"

# Having it all would mean nothing without purpose.

(For days when you need to focus on what's important)

"Having the world would mean nothing with no one to share it with" isn't a statement about relationships. The underlying theme is purpose. What would it mean to have accumulated riches, wealth and even a bunch of relationships if there was no purpose involved in any of it? You're here for a reason. And life is much more fulfilling once you find out why. Truth be told, there can be no direction and intention to any of your movement without purpose. Let's not make accumulation the sole intention of our doing as if that will lead to any life worth living. Do the hard, introspective assessment work to realize the purpose that has always been intrinsic to your being. Living for yourself isn't nearly as rewarding as living for others – not for their approval but for their betterment. Start there.

Wisdom – For Days

**Bryan Pharr**

**Thank you for reading
Wisdom – For Days!**

Make sure to leave a rating of this book
anywhere it's being sold!

# ABOUT BRYAN PHARR

**Bryan Pharr** is a motivational/inspirational speaker, writer, coach and entrepreneur who is an emerging, leading voice to his generation, preparing and equipping them for an abundant life. His message is clear: He desires that all people would come into a full knowledge of who they really are and lead lives that are full of fulfillment. As the founder of IEXIST (**becomingallthatweare.com**), a Wellness Brand and company that is geared toward the betterment of all people, Bryan is constantly working out effective ways and strategies to inform and inspire those who need it, in an effort to push them to become everything that they are.

## LET'S STAY CONNECTED:

Facebook: facebook.com/bryanpharr
Instagram: @bryanpharr
Twitter: @bryanpharr

www.ingramcontent.com/pod-product-compliance
Lightning Source LLC
Chambersburg PA
CBHW050515170426
43201CB00013B/1966